Arnold Bennett
New Thought Collection

How to Live on Twenty-Four Hours a Day

The Human Machine

Mental Efficiency

PATH NOTES PRESS

How to Live on Twenty-Four Hours a Day

First Published 1910

The Human Machine

First Published in 1925

Mental Efficiency

First Published in 1911

A *New Thought* Classic

Path Notes Press books are available for order through Ingram Press Catalogues

Printed in the United States of America

ISBN: 978-0-9975950-5-5

Disclaimer:

The book is for academic purposes only and does not dispense medical or psychological advice.

Table of Contents

How to Live on Twenty-Four Hours a Day

The Human Machine

Mental Efficiency

How to Live on Twenty-Four Hours a Day

Preface to this Edition

This preface, though placed at the beginning, as a preface must be, should be read at the end of the book.

I have received a large amount of correspondence concerning this small work, and many reviews of it--some of them nearly as long as the book itself--have been printed. But scarcely any of the comment has been adverse. Some people have objected to a frivolity of tone; but as the tone is not, in my opinion, at all frivolous, this objection did not impress me; and had no weightier reproach been put forward I might almost have been persuaded that the volume was flawless! A more serious stricture has, however, been offered--not in the press, but by sundry obviously sincere correspondents--and I must deal with it. A reference in the following pages will show that I anticipated and feared this disapprobation. The sentence against which protests have been made is as follows:--"In the majority of instances he [the typical man] does not precisely feel a passion for his business; at best he does not dislike it. He begins his business functions with some reluctance, as late as he can, and he ends them with joy, as early as he can. And his engines, while he is engaged in his business, are seldom at their full 'horse power (h.p.)'"

I am assured, in accents of unmistakable sincerity, that there are many business men--not merely those in high positions or with fine prospects, but modest subordinates with no hope of ever being much better off--who do enjoy their business functions, who do not shirk them, who do not arrive at the office as late as possible and depart as early as possible, who, in a word, put the whole of their force into their day's work and are genuinely fatigued at the end thereof.

2

I am ready to believe it. I do believe it. I know it. I always knew it. Both in London and in the provinces it has been my lot to spend long years in subordinate situations of business; and the fact did not escape me that a certain proportion of my peers showed what amounted to an honest passion for their duties, and that while engaged in those duties they were really _living_ to the fullest extent of which they were capable. But I remain convinced that these fortunate and happy individuals (happier perhaps than they guessed) did not and do not constitute a majority, or anything like a majority. I remain convinced that the majority of decent average conscientious men of business (men with aspirations and ideals) do not as a rule go home of a night genuinely tired. I remain convinced that they put not as much but as little of themselves as they conscientiously can into the earning of a livelihood, and that their vocation bores rather than interests them.

Nevertheless, I admit that the minority is of sufficient importance to merit attention, and that I ought not to have ignored it so completely as I did do. The whole difficulty of the hard-working minority was put in a single colloquial sentence by one of my correspondents. He wrote: "I am just as keen as anyone on doing something to 'exceed my programme,' but allow me to tell you that when I get home at six thirty p.m. I am not anything like so fresh as you seem to imagine."

Now I must point out that the case of the minority, who throw themselves with passion and gusto into their daily business task, is infinitely less deplorable than the case of the majority, who go half-heartedly and feebly through their official day. The former are less in need of advice "how to live." At any rate during their official day of, say, eight hours they are really alive; their engines are giving the full indicated "h.p." The other eight working hours of their day may be badly organised, or even frittered away; but it is less disastrous to waste eight hours a day than sixteen hours a day; it is better to have lived a bit than never to have lived at all. The real tragedy is the tragedy of the man who is braced to effort neither in the office nor out of it, and to this man this book is primarily addressed. "But," says the other and more fortunate man, "although my ordinary programme is bigger than his, I want to exceed my programme too! I am living a bit; I want to live more. But I really can't do another day's work on the top of my official day."

The fact is, I, the author, ought to have foreseen that I should appeal most strongly to those who already had an interest in existence. It is always the man who has tasted life who demands more of it. And it is always the man who never gets out of bed who is the most difficult to rouse.

Well, you of the minority, let us assume that the intensity of your daily money-getting will not allow you to carry out quite all the suggestions in the following pages. Some of the suggestions may yet stand. I admit that you may not be able to use the time spent on the journey home at night; but the suggestion for the journey to the office in the morning is as practicable for you as for anybody. And that weekly interval of forty hours, from Saturday to Monday, is yours just as much as the other man's, though a slight accumulation of fatigue may prevent you from employing the whole of your "h.p." upon it. There remains, then, the important portion of the three or more evenings a week. You tell me flatly that you are too tired to do anything outside your programme at night. In reply to which I tell you flatly that if your ordinary day's work is thus exhausting, then the balance of your life is wrong and must be adjusted. A man's powers ought not to be monopolised by his ordinary day's work. What, then, is to be done?

The obvious thing to do is to circumvent your ardour for your ordinary day's work by a ruse. Employ your engines in something beyond the programme before, and not after, you employ them on the programme itself. Briefly, get up earlier in the morning. You say you cannot. You say it is impossible for you to go earlier to bed of a night--to do so would upset the entire household. I do not think it is quite impossible to go to bed earlier at night. I think that if you persist in rising earlier, and the consequence is insufficiency of sleep, you will soon find a way of going to bed earlier. But my impression is that the consequences of rising earlier will not be an insufficiency of sleep. My impression, growing stronger every year, is that sleep is partly a matter of habit--and of slackness. I am convinced that most people sleep as long as they do because they are at a loss for any other diversion. How much sleep do you think is daily obtained by the powerful healthy man who daily rattles up your street in charge of Carter Patterson's van? I have consulted a doctor on this point. He is a doctor who for twenty-four years has had a large general practice in a large flourishing suburb of London, inhabited by exactly such people as you and me. He is a curt man, and his answer was curt:

"Most people sleep themselves stupid."

He went on to give his opinion that nine men out of ten would have better health and more fun out of life if they spent less time in bed.

Other doctors have confirmed this judgment, which, of course, does not apply to growing youths.

Rise an hour, an hour and a half, or even two hours earlier; and--if you must--retire earlier when you can. In the matter of exceeding programmes, you will accomplish as much in one morning hour as in two evening hours. "But," you say, "I couldn't begin without some food, and servants." Surely, my dear sir, in an age when an excellent spirit-lamp (including a saucepan) can be bought for less than a shilling, you are not

5

going to allow your highest welfare to depend upon the precarious immediate co-operation of a fellow creature! Instruct the fellow creature, whoever she may be, at night. Tell her to put a tray in a suitable position over night. On that tray two biscuits, a cup and saucer, a box of matches and a spirit-lamp; on the lamp, the saucepan; on the saucepan, the lid--but turned the wrong way up; on the reversed lid, the small teapot, containing a minute quantity of tea leaves. You will then have to strike a match--that is all. In three minutes the water boils, and you pour it into the teapot (which is already warm). In three more minutes the tea is infused. You can begin your day while drinking it. These details may seem trivial to the foolish, but to the thoughtful they will not seem trivial. The proper, wise balancing of one's whole life may depend upon the feasibility of a cup of tea at an unusual hour.

A.B.

Chapter I

The Daily Miracle

"Yes, he's one of those men that don't know how to manage. Good situation. Regular income. Quite enough for luxuries as well as needs. Not really extravagant. And yet the fellow's always in difficulties. Somehow he gets nothing out of his money. Excellent flat--half empty! Always looks as if he'd had the brokers in. New suit--old hat! Magnificent necktie--baggy trousers! Asks you to dinner: cut glass--bad mutton, or Turkish coffee--cracked cup! He can't understand it. Explanation simply is that he fritters his income away. Wish I had the half of it! I'd show him--"

So we have most of us criticised, at one time or another, in our superior way.

We are nearly all chancellors of the exchequer: it is the pride of the moment. Newspapers are full of articles explaining how to live on such-and-such a sum, and these articles provoke a correspondence whose violence proves the interest they excite. Recently, in a daily organ, a battle raged round the question whether a woman can exist nicely in the country on L85 a year. I have seen an essay, "How to live on eight shillings a week." But I have never seen an essay, "How to live on twenty-four hours a day." Yet it has been said that time is money. That proverb understates the case. Time is a great deal more than money. If you have time you can obtain money--usually. But though you have the wealth of a cloak-room attendant at the Carlton Hotel, you cannot buy yourself a minute more time than I have, or the cat by the fire has.

7

Philosophers have explained space. They have not explained time. It is the inexplicable raw material of everything. With it, all is possible; without it, nothing. The supply of time is truly a daily miracle, an affair genuinely astonishing when one examines it. You wake up in the morning, and lo! your purse is magically filled with twenty-four hours of the unmanufactured tissue of the universe of your life! It is yours. It is the most precious of possessions. A highly singular commodity, showered upon you in a manner as singular as the commodity itself!

For remark! No one can take it from you. It is unstealable. And no one receives either more or less than you receive.

Talk about an ideal democracy! In the realm of time there is no aristocracy of wealth, and no aristocracy of intellect. Genius is never rewarded by even an extra hour a day. And there is no punishment. Waste your infinitely precious commodity as much as you will, and the supply will never be withheld from you. No mysterious power will say:--"This man is a fool, if not a knave. He does not deserve time; he shall be cut off at the meter." It is more certain than consols, and payment of income is not affected by Sundays. Moreover, you cannot draw on the future. Impossible to get into debt! *You can only waste the passing moment.* You cannot waste to-morrow; it is kept for you. You cannot waste the next hour; it is kept for you.

I said the affair was a miracle. Is it not?

You have to live on this twenty-four hours of daily time. Out of it you have to spin health, pleasure, money, content, respect, and the evolution of your immortal soul. Its right use, its most effective use, is a matter of the highest urgency and of the most thrilling actuality. All depends on that. Your happiness--the elusive prize that you are all clutching for, my friends!--depends on that. Strange that the newspapers, so enterprising and up-to-date as they are, are not full of "How to live on a given income of

8

time," instead of "How to live on a given income of money"! Money is far commoner than time. When one reflects, one perceives that money is just about the commonest thing there is. It encumbers the earth in gross heaps.

If one can't contrive to live on a certain income of money, one earns a little more--or steals it, or advertises for it. One doesn't necessarily muddle one's life because one can't quite manage on a thousand pounds a year; one braces the muscles and makes it guineas, and balances the budget. But if one cannot arrange that an income of twenty-four hours a day shall exactly cover all proper items of expenditure, one does muddle one's life definitely. The supply of time, though gloriously regular, is cruelly restricted.

Which of us lives on twenty-four hours a day? And when I say "lives," I do not mean exists, nor "muddles through." Which of us is free from that uneasy feeling that the "great spending departments" of his daily life are not managed as they ought to be? Which of us is quite sure that his fine suit is not surmounted by a shameful hat, or that in attending to the crockery he has forgotten the quality of the food? Which of us is not saying to himself--which of us has not been saying to himself all his life: "I shall alter that when I have a little more time"?

We never shall have any more time. We have, and we have always had, all the time there is. It is the realisation of this profound and neglected truth (which, by the way, I have not discovered) that has led me to the minute practical examination of daily time-expenditure.

Chapter II

The Desire to Exceed One's Programme

"But," someone may remark, with the English disregard of everything except the point, "what is he driving at with his twenty-four hours a day? I have no difficulty in living on twenty-four hours a day. I do all that I want to do, and still find time to go in for newspaper competitions. Surely it is a simple affair, knowing that one has only twenty-four hours a day, to content one's self with twenty-four hours a day!"

To you, my dear sir, I present my excuses and apologies. You are precisely the man that I have been wishing to meet for about forty years. Will you kindly send me your name and address, and state your charge for telling me how you do it? Instead of me talking to you, you ought to be talking to me. Please come forward. That you exist, I am convinced, and that I have not yet encountered you is my loss. Meanwhile, until you appear, I will continue to chat with my companions in distress--that innumerable band of souls who are haunted, more or less painfully, by the feeling that the years slip by, and slip by, and slip by, and that they have not yet been able to get their lives into proper working order.

If we analyse that feeling, we shall perceive it to be, primarily, one of uneasiness, of expectation, of looking forward, of aspiration. It is a source of constant discomfort, for it behaves like a skeleton at the feast of all our enjoyments. We go to the theatre and laugh; but between the acts it raises a skinny finger at us. We rush violently for the last train, and while we are cooling a long age on the platform waiting for the last train, it promenades its bones up and down by our side and inquires: "O man, what hast thou done with thy youth? What art thou doing with thine age?" You may urge that this feeling of continuous looking forward, of aspiration, is part of life itself, and inseparable from life itself. True!

But there are degrees. A man may desire to go to Mecca. His conscience tells him that he ought to go to Mecca. He fares forth, either by the aid of Cook's, or unassisted; he may probably never reach Mecca; he may drown before he gets to Port Said; he may perish ingloriously on the coast of the Red Sea; his desire may remain eternally frustrate. Unfulfilled aspiration may always trouble him. But he will not be tormented in the same way as the man who, desiring to reach Mecca, and harried by the desire to reach Mecca, never leaves Brixton.

It is something to have left Brixton. Most of us have not left Brixton. We have not even taken a cab to Ludgate Circus and inquired from Cook's the price of a conducted tour. And our excuse to ourselves is that there are only twenty-four hours in the day.

If we further analyse our vague, uneasy aspiration, we shall, I think, see that it springs from a fixed idea that we ought to do something in addition to those things which we are loyally and morally obliged to do. We are obliged, by various codes written and unwritten, to maintain ourselves and our families (if any) in health and comfort, to pay our debts, to save, to increase our prosperity by increasing our efficiency. A task sufficiently difficult! A task which very few of us achieve! A task often beyond our skill! Yet, if we succeed in it, as we sometimes do, we are not satisfied; the skeleton is still with us.

And even when we realise that the task is beyond our skill, that our powers cannot cope with it, we feel that we should be less discontented if we gave to our powers, already overtaxed, something still further to do.

And such is, indeed, the fact. The wish to accomplish something outside their formal programme is common to all men who in the course of evolution have risen past a certain level.

Until an effort is made to satisfy that wish, the sense of uneasy waiting for something to start which has not started will remain to disturb the peace of the soul. That wish has been called by many names. It is one form of the universal desire for knowledge. And it is so strong that men whose whole lives have been given to the systematic acquirement of knowledge have been driven by it to overstep the limits of their programme in search of still more knowledge. Even Herbert Spencer, in my opinion the greatest mind that ever lived, was often forced by it into agreeable little backwaters of inquiry.

I imagine that in the majority of people who are conscious of the wish to live--that is to say, people who have intellectual curiosity--the aspiration to exceed formal programmes takes a literary shape. They would like to embark on a course of reading. Decidedly the British people are becoming more and more literary. But I would point out that literature by no means comprises the whole field of knowledge, and that the disturbing thirst to improve one's self--to increase one's knowledge--may well be slaked quite apart from literature. With the various ways of slaking I shall deal later. Here I merely point out to those who have no natural sympathy with literature that literature is not the only well.

Chapter III

Precautions Before Beginning

Now that I have succeeded (if succeeded I have) in persuading you to admit to yourself that you are constantly haunted by a suppressed dissatisfaction with your own arrangement of your daily life; and that the primal cause of that inconvenient dissatisfaction is the feeling that you are every day leaving undone something which you would like to do, and which, indeed, you are always hoping to do when you have "more time"; and now that I have drawn your attention to the glaring, dazzling truth that you never will have "more time," since you already have all the time there is--you expect me to let you into some wonderful secret by which you may at any rate approach the ideal of a perfect arrangement of the day, and by which, therefore, that haunting, unpleasant, daily disappointment of things left undone will be got rid of!

I have found no such wonderful secret. Nor do I expect to find it, nor do I expect that anyone else will ever find it. It is undiscovered. When you first began to gather my drift, perhaps there was a resurrection of hope in your breast. Perhaps you said to yourself, "This man will show me an easy, unfatiguing way of doing what I have so long in vain wished to do." Alas, no! The fact is that there is no easy way, no royal road. The path to Mecca is extremely hard and stony, and the worst of it is that you never quite get there after all.

The most important preliminary to the task of arranging one's life so that one may live fully and comfortably within one's daily budget of twenty-four hours is the calm realisation of the extreme difficulty of the task, of the sacrifices and the endless effort which it demands. I cannot too strongly insist on this.

If you imagine that you will be able to achieve your ideal by ingeniously planning out a time-table with a pen on a piece of paper, you had better give up hope at once. If you are not prepared for discouragements and disillusions; if you will not be content with a small result for a big effort, then do not begin. Lie down again and resume the uneasy doze which you call your existence.

It is very sad, is it not, very depressing and somber? And yet I think it is rather fine, too, this necessity for the tense bracing of the will before anything worth doing can be done. I rather like it myself. I feel it to be the chief thing that differentiates me from the cat by the fire.

"Well," you say, "assume that I am braced for the battle. Assume that I have carefully weighed and comprehended your ponderous remarks; how do I begin?" Dear sir, you simply begin. There is no magic method of beginning. If a man standing on the edge of a swimming-bath and wanting to jump into the cold water should ask you, "How do I begin to jump?" you would merely reply, "Just jump. Take hold of your nerves, and jump."

As I have previously said, the chief beauty about the constant supply of time is that you cannot waste it in advance. The next year, the next day, the next hour are lying ready for you, as perfect, as unspoilt, as if you had never wasted or misapplied a single moment in all your career. Which fact is very gratifying and reassuring. You can turn over a new leaf every hour if you choose. Therefore no object is served in waiting till next week, or even until to-morrow. You may fancy that the water will be warmer next week. It won't. It will be colder.

But before you begin, let me murmur a few words of warning in your private ear. Let me principally warn you against your own ardour. Ardour in well-doing is a misleading and a treacherous thing. It cries out loudly for employment; you can't satisfy it at first; it wants more and more; it is eager to move mountains and divert the course of rivers. It isn't content till it perspires. And then, too often, when it feels the perspiration on its brow, it wearies all of a sudden and dies, without even putting itself to the trouble of saying, "I've had enough of this."

Beware of undertaking too much at the start. Be content with quite a little. Allow for accidents. Allow for human nature, especially your own.

A failure or so, in itself, would not matter, if it did not incur a loss of self-esteem and of self-confidence. But just as nothing succeeds like success, so nothing fails like failure. Most people who are ruined are ruined by attempting too much. Therefore, in setting out on the immense enterprise of living fully and comfortably within the narrow limits of twenty-four hours a day, let us avoid at any cost the risk of an early failure. I will not agree that, in this business at any rate, a glorious failure is better than a petty success. I am all for the petty success. A glorious failure leads to nothing; a petty success may lead to a success that is not petty.

So let us begin to examine the budget of the day's time. You say your day is already full to overflowing. How? You actually spend in earning your livelihood--how much? Seven hours, on the average? And in actual sleep, seven? I will add two hours, and be generous. And I will defy you to account to me on the spur of the moment for the other eight hours.

Chapter IV

The Cause of the Trouble

In order to come to grips at once with the question of time-expenditure in all its actuality, I must choose an individual case for examination. I can only deal with one case, and that case cannot be the average case, because there is no such case as the average case, just as there is no such man as the average man. Every man and every man's case is special.

But if I take the case of a Londoner who works in an office, whose office hours are from ten to six, and who spends fifty minutes morning and night in travelling between his house door and his office door, I shall have got as near to the average as facts permit. There are men who have to work longer for a living, but there are others who do not have to work so long.

Fortunately the financial side of existence does not interest us here; for our present purpose the clerk at a pound a week is exactly as well off as the millionaire in Carlton House-terrace.

Now the great and profound mistake which my typical man makes in regard to his day is a mistake of general attitude, a mistake which vitiates and weakens two-thirds of his energies and interests. In the majority of instances he does not precisely feel a passion for his business; at best he does not dislike it. He begins his business functions with reluctance, as late as he can, and he ends them with joy, as early as he can. And his engines while he is engaged in his business are seldom at their full "h.p."

(I know that I shall be accused by angry readers of traducing the city worker; but I am pretty thoroughly acquainted with the City, and I stick to what I say.)

Yet in spite of all this he persists in looking upon those hours from ten to six as "the day," to which the ten hours preceding them and the six hours following them are nothing but a prologue and epilogue. Such an attitude, unconscious though it be, of course kills his interest in the odd sixteen hours, with the result that, even if he does not waste them, he does not count them; he regards them simply as margin.

This general attitude is utterly illogical and unhealthy, since it formally gives the central prominence to a patch of time and a bunch of activities which the man's one idea is to "get through" and have "done with." If a man makes two-thirds of his existence subservient to one-third, for which admittedly he has no absolutely feverish zest, how can he hope to live fully and completely? He cannot.

If my typical man wishes to live fully and completely he must, in his mind, arrange a day within a day. And this inner day, a Chinese box in a larger Chinese box, must begin at 6 p.m. and end at 10 a.m. It is a day of sixteen hours; and during all these sixteen hours he has nothing whatever to do but cultivate his body and his soul and his fellow men. During those sixteen hours he is free; he is not a wage-earner; he is not preoccupied with monetary cares; he is just as good as a man with a private income. This must be his attitude. And his attitude is all important. His success in life (much more important than the amount of estate upon what his executors will have to pay estate duty) depends on it.

What? You say that full energy given to those sixteen hours will lessen the value of the business eight? Not so. On the contrary, it will assuredly increase the value of the business eight. One of the chief things which my typical man has to learn is that the mental faculties are capable of a continuous hard activity; they do not tire like an arm or a leg. All they want is change--not rest, except in sleep.

I shall now examine the typical man's current method of employing the sixteen hours that are entirely his, beginning with his uprising. I will merely indicate things which he does and which I think he ought not to do, postponing my suggestions for "planting" the times which I shall have cleared--as a settler clears spaces in a forest.

In justice to him I must say that he wastes very little time before he leaves the house in the morning at 9.10. In too many houses he gets up at nine, breakfasts between 9.7 and 9.9 1/2, and then bolts. But immediately he bangs the front door his mental faculties, which are tireless, become idle. He walks to the station in a condition of mental coma. Arrived there, he usually has to wait for the train. On hundreds of suburban stations every morning you see men calmly strolling up and down platforms while railway companies unblushingly rob them of time, which is more than money. Hundreds of thousands of hours are thus lost every day simply because my typical man thinks so little of time that it has never occurred to him to take quite easy precautions against the risk of its loss.

He has a solid coin of time to spend every day--call it a sovereign. He must get change for it, and in getting change he is content to lose heavily.

Supposing that in selling him a ticket the company said, "We will change you a sovereign, but we shall charge you three halfpence for doing so," what would my typical man exclaim? Yet that is the equivalent of what the company does when it robs him of five minutes twice a day.

You say I am dealing with minutiae. I am. And later on I will justify myself.

Now will you kindly buy your paper and step into the train?

Chapter V

Tennis and the Immortal Soul

You get into the morning train with your newspaper, and you calmly and majestically give yourself up to your newspaper. You do not hurry. You know you have at least half an hour of security in front of you. As your glance lingers idly at the advertisements of shipping and of songs on the outer pages, your air is the air of a leisured man, wealthy in time, of a man from some planet where there are a hundred and twenty-four hours a day instead of twenty-four. I am an impassioned reader of newspapers. I read five English and two French dailies, and the news-agents alone know how many weeklies, regularly. I am obliged to mention this personal fact lest I should be accused of a prejudice against newspapers when I say that I object to the reading of newspapers in the morning train. Newspapers are produced with rapidity, to be read with rapidity. There is no place in my daily programme for newspapers. I read them as I may in odd moments. But I do read them. The idea of devoting to them thirty or forty consecutive minutes of wonderful solitude (for nowhere can one more perfectly immerse one's self in one's self than in a compartment full of silent, withdrawn, smoking males) is to me repugnant. I cannot possibly allow you to scatter priceless pearls of time with such Oriental lavishness. You are not the Shah of time. Let me respectfully remind you that you have no more time than I have. No newspaper reading in trains! I have already "put by" about three-quarters of an hour for use.

Now you reach your office. And I abandon you there till six o'clock. I am aware that you have nominally an hour (often in reality an hour and a half) in the midst of the day, less than half of which time is given to eating. But I will leave you all that to spend as you choose. You may read your newspapers then.

I meet you again as you emerge from your office. You are pale and tired. At any rate, your wife says you are pale, and you give her to understand that you are tired. During the journey home you have been gradually working up the tired feeling. The tired feeling hangs heavy over the mighty suburbs of London like a virtuous and melancholy cloud, particularly in winter. You don't eat immediately on your arrival home. But in about an hour or so you feel as if you could sit up and take a little nourishment. And you do. Then you smoke, seriously; you see friends; you potter; you play cards; you flirt with a book; you note that old age is creeping on; you take a stroll; you caress the piano.... By Jove! a quarter past eleven. You then devote quite forty minutes to thinking about going to bed; and it is conceivable that you are acquainted with a genuinely good whisky. At last you go to bed, exhausted by the day's work. Six hours, probably more, have gone since you left the office--gone like a dream, gone like magic, unaccountably gone!

That is a fair sample case. But you say: "It's all very well for you to talk. A man _is_ tired. A man must see his friends. He can't always be on the stretch." Just so. But when you arrange to go to the theatre (especially with a pretty woman) what happens? You rush to the suburbs; you spare no toil to make yourself glorious in fine raiment; you rush back to town in another train; you keep yourself on the stretch for four hours, if not five; you take her home; you take yourself home. You don't spend three-quarters of an hour in "thinking about" going to bed. You go. Friends and fatigue have equally been forgotten, and the evening has seemed so exquisitely long (or perhaps too short)! And do you remember that time when you were persuaded to sing in the chorus of the amateur operatic society, and slaved

21

two hours every other night for three months? Can you deny that when you have something definite to look forward to at eventide, something that is to employ all your energy--the thought of that something gives a glow and a more intense vitality to the whole day?

What I suggest is that at six o'clock you look facts in the face and admit that you are not tired (because you are not, you know), and that you arrange your evening so that it is not cut in the middle by a meal. By so doing you will have a clear expanse of at least three hours. I do not suggest that you should employ three hours every night of your life in using up your mental energy. But I do suggest that you might, for a commencement, employ an hour and a half every other evening in some important and consecutive cultivation of the mind. You will still be left with three evenings for friends, bridge, tennis, domestic scenes, odd reading, pipes, gardening, pottering, and prize competitions. You will still have the terrific wealth of forty-five hours between 2 p.m. Saturday and 10 a.m. Monday. If you persevere you will soon want to pass four evenings, and perhaps five, in some sustained endeavour to be genuinely alive. And you will fall out of that habit of muttering to yourself at 11.15 p.m., "Time to be thinking about going to bed." The man who begins to go to bed forty minutes before he opens his bedroom door is bored; that is to say, he is not living.

But remember, at the start, those ninety nocturnal minutes thrice a week must be the most important minutes in the ten thousand and eighty. They must be sacred, quite as sacred as a dramatic rehearsal or a tennis match. Instead of saying, "Sorry I can't see you, old chap, but I have to run off to the tennis club," you must say, "...but I have to work." This, I admit, is intensely difficult to say. Tennis is so much more urgent than the immortal soul.

Chapter VI
Remember Human Nature

I have incidentally mentioned the vast expanse of forty-four hours between leaving business at 2 p.m. on Saturday and returning to business at 10 a.m. on Monday. And here I must touch on the point whether the week should consist of six days or of seven. For many years--in fact, until I was approaching forty--my own week consisted of seven days. I was constantly being informed by older and wiser people that more work, more genuine living, could be got out of six days than out of seven.

And it is certainly true that now, with one day in seven in which I follow no programme and make no effort save what the caprice of the moment dictates, I appreciate intensely the moral value of a weekly rest. Nevertheless, had I my life to arrange over again, I would do again as I have done. Only those who have lived at the full stretch seven days a week for a long time can appreciate the full beauty of a regular recurring idleness. Moreover, I am ageing. And it is a question of age. In cases of abounding youth and exceptional energy and desire for effort I should say unhesitatingly: Keep going, day in, day out.

But in the average case I should say: Confine your formal programme (super-programme, I mean) to six days a week. If you find yourself wishing to extend it, extend it, but only in proportion to your wish; and count the time extra as a windfall, not as regular income, so that you can return to a six-day programme without the sensation of being poorer, of being a backslider.

Let us now see where we stand. So far we have marked for saving out of the waste of days, half an hour at least on six mornings a week, and one hour and a half on three evenings a week. Total, seven hours and a half a week.

I propose to be content with that seven hours and a half for the present. "What?" you cry. "You pretend to show us how to live, and you only deal with seven hours and a half out of a hundred and sixty-eight! Are you going to perform a miracle with your seven hours and a half?" Well, not to mince the matter, I am--if you will kindly let me! That is to say, I am going to ask you to attempt an experience which, while perfectly natural and explicable, has all the air of a miracle. My contention is that the full use of those seven-and-a-half hours will quicken the whole life of the week, add zest to it, and increase the interest which you feel in even the most banal occupations. You practise physical exercises for a mere ten minutes morning and evening, and yet you are not astonished when your physical health and strength are beneficially affected every hour of the day, and your whole physical outlook changed. Why should you be astonished that an average of over an hour a day given to the mind should permanently and completely enliven the whole activity of the mind?

More time might assuredly be given to the cultivation of one's self. And in proportion as the time was longer the results would be greater. But I prefer to begin with what looks like a trifling effort.

It is not really a trifling effort, as those will discover who have yet to essay it. To "clear" even seven hours and a half from the jungle is passably difficult. For some sacrifice has to be made. One may have spent one's time badly, but one did spend it; one

24

did do something with it, however ill-advised that something may have been. To do something else means a change of habits.

And habits are the very dickens to change! Further, any change, even a change for the better, is always accompanied by drawbacks and discomforts. If you imagine that you will be able to devote seven hours and a half a week to serious, continuous effort, and still live your old life, you are mistaken. I repeat that some sacrifice, and an immense deal of volition, will be necessary. And it is because I know the difficulty, it is because I know the almost disastrous effect of failure in such an enterprise, that I earnestly advise a very humble beginning. You must safeguard your self-respect. Self-respect is at the root of all purposefulness, and a failure in an enterprise deliberately planned deals a desperate wound at one's self-respect. Hence I iterate and reiterate: Start quietly, unostentatiously.

When you have conscientiously given seven hours and a half a week to the cultivation of your vitality for three months--then you may begin to sing louder and tell yourself what wondrous things you are capable of doing.

Before coming to the method of using the indicated hours, I have one final suggestion to make. That is, as regards the evenings, to allow much more than an hour and a half in which to do the work of an hour and a half. Remember the chance of accidents. Remember human nature. And give yourself, say, from 9 to 11.30 for your task of ninety minutes.

Chapter VII
Controlling the Mind

People say: "One can't help one's thoughts." But one can. The control of the thinking machine is perfectly possible. And since nothing whatever happens to us outside our own brain; since nothing hurts us or gives us pleasure except within the brain, the supreme importance of being able to control what goes on in that mysterious brain is patent. This idea is one of the oldest platitudes, but it is a platitude whose profound truth and urgency most people live and die without realising. People complain of the lack of power to concentrate, not witting that they may acquire the power, if they choose.

And without the power to concentrate--that is to say, without the power to dictate to the brain its task and to ensure obedience--true life is impossible. Mind control is the first element of a full existence.

Hence, it seems to me, the first business of the day should be to put the mind through its paces. You look after your body, inside and out; you run grave danger in hacking hairs off your skin; you employ a whole army of individuals, from the milkman to the pig-killer, to enable you to bribe your stomach into decent behaviour. Why not devote a little attention to the far more delicate machinery of the mind, especially as you will require no extraneous aid? It is for this portion of the art and craft of living

26

that I have reserved the time from the moment of quitting your door to the moment of arriving at your office.

"What? I am to cultivate my mind in the street, on the platform, in the train, and in the crowded street again?" Precisely. Nothing simpler! No tools required! Not even a book. Nevertheless, the affair is not easy.

When you leave your house, concentrate your mind on a subject (no matter what, to begin with). You will not have gone ten yards before your mind has skipped away under your very eyes and is larking round the corner with another subject.

Bring it back by the scruff of the neck. Ere you have reached the station you will have brought it back about forty times. Do not despair. Continue. Keep it up. You will succeed. You cannot by any chance fail if you persevere. It is idle to pretend that your mind is incapable of concentration. Do you not remember that morning when you received a disquieting letter which demanded a very carefully-worded answer? How you kept your mind steadily on the subject of the answer, without a second's intermission, until you reached your office; whereupon you instantly sat down and wrote the answer? That was a case in which _you_ were roused by circumstances to such a degree of vitality that you were able to dominate your mind like a tyrant. You would have no trifling. You insisted that its work should be done, and its work was done.

By the regular practice of concentration (as to which there is no secret--save the secret of perseverance) you can tyrannise over your mind (which is not the highest part of _you_) every hour of the day, and in no matter what place. The exercise is a very convenient one. If you got into your morning train with a pair of dumb-bells for your muscles or an encyclopedia in ten volumes for your learning, you would probably excite remark. But as you walk in the street, or sit in the corner of the compartment

27

behind a pipe, or "strap-hang" on the Subterranean, who is to know that you are engaged in the most important of daily acts? What asinine boor can laugh at you?

I do not care what you concentrate on, so long as you concentrate. It is the mere disciplining of the thinking machine that counts. But still, you may as well kill two birds with one stone, and concentrate on something useful. I suggest--it is only a suggestion--a little chapter of Marcus Aurelius or Epictetus.

Do not, I beg, shy at their names. For myself, I know nothing more "actual," more bursting with plain common-sense, applicable to the daily life of plain persons like you and me (who hate airs, pose, and nonsense) than Marcus Aurelius or Epictetus. Read a chapter--and so short they are, the chapters!-- in the evening and concentrate on it the next morning. You will see.

Yes, my friend, it is useless for you to try to disguise the fact. I can hear your brain like a telephone at my ear. You are saying to yourself: "This fellow was doing pretty well up to his seventh chapter. He had begun to interest me faintly. But what he says about thinking in trains, and concentration, and so on, is not for me. It may be well enough for some folks, but it isn't in my line."

It is for you, I passionately repeat; it is for you. Indeed, you are the very man I am aiming at.

Throw away the suggestion, and you throw away the most precious suggestion that was ever offered to you. It is not my suggestion. It is the suggestion of the most sensible, practical, hard-headed men who have walked the earth. I only give it you at second-hand. Try it. Get your mind in hand. And see how the process cures half the evils of life--especially worry, that miserable, avoidable, shameful disease--worry!

Chapter VIII
The Reflective Mood

The exercise of concentrating the mind (to which at least half an hour a day should be given) is a mere preliminary, like scales on the piano. Having acquired power over that most unruly member of one's complex organism, one has naturally to put it to the yoke. Useless to possess an obedient mind unless one profits to the furthest possible degree by its obedience. A prolonged primary course of study is indicated.

Now as to what this course of study should be there cannot be any question; there never has been any question. All the sensible people of all ages are agreed upon it. And it is not literature, nor is it any other art, nor is it history, nor is it any science. It is the study of one's self. Man, know thyself. These words are so hackneyed that verily I blush to write them. Yet they must be written, for they need to be written. (I take back my blush, being ashamed of it.) Man, know thyself. I say it out loud. The phrase is one of those phrases with which everyone is familiar, of which everyone acknowledges the value, and which only the most sagacious put into practice. I don't know why. I am entirely convinced that what is more than anything else lacking in the life of the average well-intentioned man of to-day is the reflective mood.

We do not reflect. I mean that we do not reflect upon genuinely important things; upon the problem of our happiness, upon the main direction in which we are going, upon what life is giving to us, upon the share which reason has (or has not) in determining our actions, and upon the relation between our principles and our conduct.

And yet you are in search of happiness, are you not? Have you discovered it?

The chances are that you have not. The chances are that you have already come to believe that happiness is unattainable. But men have attained it. And they have attained it by realising that happiness does not spring from the procuring of physical or mental pleasure, but from the development of reason and the adjustment of conduct to principles.

I suppose that you will not have the audacity to deny this. And if you admit it, and still devote no part of your day to the deliberate consideration of your reason, principles, and conduct, you admit also that while striving for a certain thing you are regularly leaving undone the one act which is necessary to the attainment of that thing.

Now, shall I blush, or will you?

Do not fear that I mean to thrust certain principles upon your attention. I care not (in this place) what your principles are. Your principles may induce you to believe in the righteousness of burglary. I don't mind. All I urge is that a life in which conduct does not fairly well accord with principles is a silly life; and that conduct can only be made to accord with principles by means of daily examination, reflection, and resolution. What leads to the permanent sorrowfulness of burglars is that their principles are contrary to burglary. If they genuinely believed in the moral excellence of burglary, penal servitude would simply mean so many happy years for them; all martyrs are happy, because their conduct and their principles agree.

As for reason (which makes conduct, and is not unconnected with the making of principles), it plays a far smaller part in our lives than we fancy. We are supposed to be reasonable but we are much more instinctive than reasonable. And the less we reflect, the less reasonable we shall be. The next time you get cross with the waiter because your steak is over-cooked, ask reason to step into the cabinet-room of your mind, and consult her. She will probably tell you that the waiter did not cook the steak, and had no control over the cooking of the steak; and that even if he alone was to blame, you accomplished nothing good by getting cross; you merely lost your dignity, looked a fool in the eyes of sensible men, and soured the waiter, while producing no effect whatever on the steak.

The result of this consultation with reason (for which she makes no charge) will be that when once more your steak is over-cooked you will treat the waiter as a fellow-creature, remain quite calm in a kindly spirit, and politely insist on having a fresh steak. The gain will be obvious and solid.

In the formation or modification of principles, and the practice of conduct, much help can be derived from printed books (issued at sixpence each and upwards). I mentioned in my last chapter Marcus Aurelius and Epictetus. Certain even more widely known works will occur at once to the memory. I may also mention Pascal, La Bruyere, and Emerson. For myself, you do not catch me travelling without my Marcus Aurelius. Yes, books are valuable. But not reading of books will take the place of a daily, candid, honest examination of what one has recently done, and what one is about to do--of a steady looking at one's self in the face (disconcerting though the sight may be).

When shall this important business be accomplished? The solitude of the evening journey home appears to me to be suitable for it. A reflective mood naturally follows the exertion of having earned the day's living. Of course if, instead of attending to an elementary and profoundly important duty, you prefer to read the paper (which you might just as well read while waiting for your dinner) I have nothing to say. But attend to it at some time of the day you must. I now come to the evening hours.

Chapter IX

Interest in the Arts

Many people pursue a regular and uninterrupted course of idleness in the evenings because they think that there is no alternative to idleness but the study of literature; and they do not happen to have a taste for literature. This is a great mistake.

Of course it is impossible, or at any rate very difficult, properly to study anything whatever without the aid of printed books. But if you desire to understand the deeper depths of bridge or of boat-sailing you would not be deterred by your lack of interest in literature from reading the best books on bridge or boat-sailing. We must, therefore, distinguish between literature, and books treating of subjects not literary. I shall come to literature in due course.

Let me now remark to those who have never read Meredith, and who are capable of being unmoved by a discussion as to whether Mr. Stephen Phillips is or is not a true poet, that they are perfectly within their rights. It is not a crime not to love literature. It is not a sign of imbecility. The mandarins of literature will order out to instant execution the unfortunate individual who does not comprehend, say, the influence of Wordsworth on Tennyson. But that is only their impudence. Where would they be, I wonder, if requested to explain the influences that went to make Tschaikowsky's "Pathetic Symphony"?

There are enormous fields of knowledge quite outside literature which will yield magnificent results to cultivators. For example (since I have just mentioned the most popular piece of high-class music in England to-day), I am reminded that the Promenade Concerts begin in August. You go to them. You smoke your cigar or cigarette (and I regret to say that you strike your matches during the soft bars of the "Lohengrin" overture), and you enjoy the music. But you say you cannot play the piano or the fiddle, or even the banjo; that you know nothing of music.

What does that matter? That you have a genuine taste for music is proved by the fact that, in order to fill his hall with you and your peers, the conductor is obliged to provide programmes from which bad music is almost entirely excluded (a change from the old Covent Garden days!).

Now surely your inability to perform "The Maiden's Prayer" on a piano need not prevent you from making yourself familiar with the construction of the orchestra to which you listen a couple of nights a week during a couple of months! As things are, you probably think of the orchestra as a heterogeneous mass of instruments producing a confused agreeable mass of sound. You do not listen for details because you have never trained your ears to listen to details.

If you were asked to name the instruments which play the great theme at the beginning of the C minor symphony you could not name them for your life's sake. Yet you admire the C minor symphony. It has thrilled you. It will thrill you again. You have even talked about it, in an expansive mood, to that lady--you know whom I mean. And all you can positively state about the C minor symphony is that Beethoven composed it and that it is a "jolly fine thing."

Now, if you have read, say, Mr. Krehbiel's "How to Listen to Music" (which can be got at any bookseller's for less than the price of a stall at the Alhambra, and which contains photographs of all the orchestral instruments and plans of the arrangement of orchestras) you would next go to a promenade concert with an astonishing intensification of interest in it. Instead of a confused mass, the orchestra would appear to you as what it is--a marvellously balanced organism whose various groups of members each have a different and an indispensable function. You would spy out the instruments, and listen for their respective sounds. You would know the gulf that separates a French horn from an English horn, and you would perceive why a player of the hautboy gets higher wages than a fiddler, though the fiddle is the more difficult instrument. You would _live_ at a promenade concert, whereas previously you had merely existed there in a state of beatific coma, like a baby gazing at a bright object.

The foundations of a genuine, systematic knowledge of music might be laid. You might specialise your inquiries either on a particular form of music (such as the symphony), or on the works of a particular composer. At the end of a year of forty-eight weeks of three brief evenings each, combined with a study of programmes and attendances at concerts chosen out of your increasing knowledge, you would really know something about music, even though you were as far off as ever from jangling "The Maiden's Prayer" on the piano.

"But I hate music!" you say. My dear sir, I respect you.

What applies to music applies to the other arts. I might mention Mr. Clermont Witt's "How to Look at Pictures," or Mr. Russell Sturgis's "How to Judge Architecture," as beginnings (merely beginnings) of systematic vitalising knowledge in other arts, the materials for whose study abound in London.

"I hate all the arts!" you say. My dear sir, I respect you more and more. I will deal with your case next, before coming to literature.

35

Chapter X

Nothing in Life is Humdrum

Art is a great thing. But it is not the greatest. The most important of all perceptions is the continual perception of cause and effect--in other words, the perception of the continuous development of the universe--in still other words, the perception of the course of evolution. When one has thoroughly got imbued into one's head the leading truth that nothing happens without a cause, one grows not only large-minded, but large-hearted.

It is hard to have one's watch stolen, but one reflects that the thief of the watch became a thief from causes of heredity and environment which are as interesting as they are scientifically comprehensible; and one buys another watch, if not with joy, at any rate with a philosophy that makes bitterness impossible. One loses, in the study of cause and effect, that absurd air which so many people have of being always shocked and pained by the curiousness of life. Such people live amid human nature as if human nature were a foreign country full of awful foreign customs. But, having reached maturity, one ought surely to be ashamed of being a stranger in a strange land!

The study of cause and effect, while it lessens the painfulness of life, adds to life's picturesqueness. The man to whom evolution is but a name looks at the sea as a grandiose, monotonous spectacle, which he can witness in August for three shillings third-class return. The man who is imbued with the idea of development, of continuous cause and effect, perceives in the sea an element which in the day-before-yesterday of geology was vapour, which yesterday was boiling, and which to-morrow will inevitably be ice.

He perceives that a liquid is merely something on its way to be solid, and he is penetrated by a sense of the tremendous, changeful picturesqueness of life. Nothing will afford a more durable satisfaction than the constantly cultivated appreciation of this. It is the end of all science.

Cause and effect are to be found everywhere. Rents went up in Shepherd's Bush. It was painful and shocking that rents should go up in Shepherd's Bush. But to a certain point we are all scientific students of cause and effect, and there was not a clerk lunching at a Lyons Restaurant who did not scientifically put two and two together and see in the (once) Two-penny Tube the cause of an excessive demand for wigwams in Shepherd's Bush, and in the excessive demand for wigwams the cause of the increase in the price of wigwams.

"Simple!" you say, disdainfully. Everything--the whole complex movement of the universe--is as simple as that--when you can sufficiently put two and two together. And, my dear sir, perhaps you happen to be an estate agent's clerk, and you hate the arts, and you want to foster your immortal soul, and you can't be interested in your business because it's so humdrum.

Nothing is humdrum.

The tremendous, changeful picturesqueness of life is marvellously shown in an estate agent's office. What! There was a block of traffic in Oxford Street; to avoid the block people actually began to travel under the cellars and drains, and the result was a rise of rents in Shepherd's Bush! And you say that isn't picturesque! Suppose you were to study, in this spirit, the property question in London for an hour and a half every other evening. Would it not give zest to your business, and transform your whole life?

You would arrive at more difficult problems. And you would be able to tell us why, as the natural result of cause and effect, the longest straight street in London is about a yard and a half in length, while the longest absolutely straight street in Paris extends for miles. I think you will admit that in an estate agent's clerk I have not chosen an example that specially favours my theories.

You are a bank clerk, and you have not read that breathless romance (disguised as a scientific study), Walter Bagehot's "Lombard Street"? Ah, my dear sir, if you had begun with that, and followed it up for ninety minutes every other evening, how enthralling your business would be to you, and how much more clearly you would understand human nature.

You are "penned in town," but you love excursions to the country and the observation of wild life--certainly a heart-enlarging diversion. Why don't you walk out of your house door, in your slippers, to the nearest gas lamp of a night with a butterfly net, and observe the wild life of common and rare moths that is beating about it, and co-ordinate the knowledge thus obtained and build a superstructure on it, and at last get to know something about something?

You need not be devoted to the arts, not to literature, in order to live fully.

The whole field of daily habit and scene is waiting to satisfy that curiosity which means life, and the satisfaction of which means an understanding heart.

I promised to deal with your case, O man who hates art and literature, and I have dealt with it. I now come to the case of the person, happily very common, who does "like reading."

Chapter XI
Serious Reading

Novels are excluded from "serious reading," so that the man who, bent on self-improvement, has been deciding to devote ninety minutes three times a week to a complete study of the works of Charles Dickens will be well advised to alter his plans. The reason is not that novels are not serious--some of the great literature of the world is in the form of prose fiction--the reason is that bad novels ought not to be read, and that good novels never demand any appreciable mental application on the part of the reader. It is only the bad parts of Meredith's novels that are difficult. A good novel rushes you forward like a skiff down a stream, and you arrive at the end, perhaps breathless, but unexhausted. The best novels involve the least strain. Now in the cultivation of the mind one of the most important factors is precisely the feeling of strain, of difficulty, of a task which one part of you is anxious to achieve and another part of you is anxious to shirk; and that feeling cannot be got in facing a novel. You do not set your teeth in order to read "Anna Karenina." Therefore, though you should read novels, you should not read them in those ninety minutes.

Imaginative poetry produces a far greater mental strain than novels. It produces probably the severest strain of any form of literature. It is the highest form of literature. It yields the highest form of pleasure, and teaches the highest form of wisdom. In a word, there is nothing to compare with it. I say this with sad consciousness of the fact that the majority of people do not read poetry.

I am persuaded that many excellent persons, if they were confronted with the alternatives of reading "Paradise Lost" and going round Trafalgar Square at noonday on their knees in sack-cloth, would choose the ordeal of public ridicule. Still, I will never cease advising my friends and enemies to read poetry before anything.

If poetry is what is called "a sealed book" to you, begin by reading Hazlitt's famous essay on the nature of "poetry in general." It is the best thing of its kind in English, and no one who has read it can possibly be under the misapprehension that poetry is a mediaeval torture, or a mad elephant, or a gun that will go off by itself and kill at forty paces. Indeed, it is difficult to imagine the mental state of the man who, after reading Hazlitt's essay, is not urgently desirous of reading some poetry before his next meal. If the essay so inspires you I would suggest that you make a commencement with purely narrative poetry.

There is an infinitely finer English novel, written by a woman, than anything by George Eliot or the Brontes, or even Jane Austen, which perhaps you have not read. Its title is "Aurora Leigh," and its author E.B. Browning. It happens to be written in verse, and to contain a considerable amount of genuinely fine poetry. Decide to read that book through, even if you die for it. Forget that it is fine poetry. Read it simply for the story and the social ideas. And when you have done, ask yourself honestly whether you still dislike poetry. I have known more than one person to whom "Aurora Leigh" has been the means of proving that in assuming they hated poetry they were entirely mistaken.

Of course, if, after Hazlitt, and such an experiment made in the light of Hazlitt, you are finally assured that there is something in you which is antagonistic to poetry, you must be content with history or philosophy. I shall regret it, yet not inconsolably. "The Decline and Fall" is not to be named in the same day with "Paradise Lost," but it is a vastly pretty thing; and Herbert Spencer's "First Principles" simply laughs at the claims of poetry and refuses to be accepted as aught but the most majestic product of any human mind. I do not suggest that either of these works is suitable for a tyro in mental strains. But I see no reason why any man of average intelligence should not, after a year of continuous reading, be fit to assault the supreme masterpieces of history or philosophy. The great convenience of masterpieces is that they are so astonishingly lucid.

I suggest no particular work as a start. The attempt would be futile in the space of my command. But I have two general suggestions of a certain importance. The first is to define the direction and scope of your efforts. Choose a limited period, or a limited subject, or a single author. Say to yourself: "I will know something about the French Revolution, or the rise of railways, or the works of John Keats." And during a given period, to be settled beforehand, confine yourself to your choice. There is much pleasure to be derived from being a specialist.

The second suggestion is to think as well as to read. I know people who read and read, and for all the good it does them they might just as well cut bread-and-butter. They take to reading as better men take to drink. They fly through the shires of literature on a motor-car, their sole object being motion. They will tell you how many books they have read in a year.

Unless you give at least forty-five minutes to careful, fatiguing reflection (it is an awful bore at first) upon what you are reading, your ninety minutes of a night are chiefly wasted. This means that your pace will be slow.

Never mind.

Forget the goal; think only of the surrounding country; and after a period, perhaps when you least expect it, you will suddenly find yourself in a lovely town on a hill.

Chapter XII

Dangers to Avoid

I cannot terminate these hints, often, I fear, too didactic and abrupt, upon the full use of one's time to the great end of living (as distinguished from vegetating) without briefly referring to certain dangers which lie in wait for the sincere aspirant towards life. The first is the terrible danger of becoming that most odious and least supportable of persons--a prig. Now a prig is a pert fellow who gives himself airs of superior wisdom. A prig is a pompous fool who has gone out for a ceremonial walk, and without knowing it has lost an important part of his attire, namely, his sense of humour. A prig is a tedious individual who, having made a discovery, is so impressed by his discovery that he is capable of being gravely displeased because the entire world is not also impressed by it. Unconsciously to become a prig is an easy and a fatal thing.

Hence, when one sets forth on the enterprise of using all one's time, it is just as well to remember that one's own time, and not other people's time, is the material with which one has to deal; that the earth rolled on pretty comfortably before one began to balance a budget of the hours, and that it will continue to roll on pretty comfortably whether or not one succeeds in one's new role of chancellor of the exchequer of time. It is as well not to chatter too much about what one is doing, and not to betray a too-pained sadness at the spectacle of a whole world deliberately wasting so many hours out of every day, and therefore never

43

really living. It will be found, ultimately, that in taking care of one's self one has quite all one can do.

Another danger is the danger of being tied to a programme like a slave to a chariot. One's programme must not be allowed to run away with one. It must be respected, but it must not be worshipped as a fetish. A programme of daily employ is not a religion.

This seems obvious. Yet I know men whose lives are a burden to themselves and a distressing burden to their relatives and friends simply because they have failed to appreciate the obvious. "Oh, no," I have heard the martyred wife exclaim, "Arthur always takes the dog out for exercise at eight o'clock and he always begins to read at a quarter to nine. So it's quite out of the question that we should..." etc., etc. And the note of absolute finality in that plaintive voice reveals the unsuspected and ridiculous tragedy of a career.

On the other hand, a programme is a programme. And unless it is treated with deference it ceases to be anything but a poor joke. To treat one's programme with exactly the right amount of deference, to live with not too much and not too little elasticity, is scarcely the simple affair it may appear to the inexperienced.

And still another danger is the danger of developing a policy of rush, of being gradually more and more obsessed by what one has to do next. In this way one may come to exist as in a prison, and one's life may cease to be one's own. One may take the dog out for a walk at eight o'clock, and meditate the whole time on the fact that one must begin to read at a quarter to nine, and that one must not be late.

And the occasional deliberate breaking of one's programme will not help to mend matters. The evil springs not from persisting without elasticity in what one has attempted, but from originally attempting too much, from filling one's programme till it runs over. The only cure is to reconstitute the programme, and to attempt less.

But the appetite for knowledge grows by what it feeds on, and there are men who come to like a constant breathless hurry of endeavour. Of them it may be said that a constant breathless hurry is better than an eternal doze.

In any case, if the programme exhibits a tendency to be oppressive, and yet one wishes not to modify it, an excellent palliative is to pass with exaggerated deliberation from one portion of it to another; for example, to spend five minutes in perfect mental quiescence between chaining up the St. Bernard and opening the book; in other words, to waste five minutes with the entire consciousness of wasting them.

The last, and chiefest danger which I would indicate, is one to which I have already referred--the risk of a failure at the commencement of the enterprise.

I must insist on it.

A failure at the commencement may easily kill outright the newborn impulse towards a complete vitality, and therefore every precaution should be observed to avoid it. The impulse must not be over-taxed. Let the pace of the first lap be even absurdly slow, but let it be as regular as possible.

And, having once decided to achieve a certain task, achieve it at all costs of tedium and distaste. The gain in self-confidence of having accomplished a tiresome labour is immense.

Finally, in choosing the first occupations of those evening hours, be guided by nothing whatever but your taste and natural inclination.

It is a fine thing to be a walking encyclopedia of philosophy, but if you happen to have no liking for philosophy, and to have a like for the natural history of street-cries, much better leave philosophy alone, and take to street-cries.

The Human Machine

Chapter I

Taking Oneself for Granted

There are men who are capable of loving a machine more deeply than they can love a woman. They are among the happiest men on earth. This is not a sneer meanly shot from cover at women. It is simply a statement of notorious fact. Men who worry themselves to distraction over the perfecting of a machine are indubitably blessed beyond their kind. Most of us have known such men. Yesterday they were constructing motorcars. But to-day aeroplanes are in the air--or, at any rate, they ought to be, according to the inventors. Watch the inventors. Invention is not usually their principal business. They must invent in their spare time. They must invent before breakfast, invent in the Strand between Lyons's and the office, invent after dinner, invent on Sundays. See with what ardour they rush home of a night! See how they seize a half-holiday, like hungry dogs a bone! They don't want golf, bridge, limericks, novels, illustrated magazines, clubs, whisky, starting-prices, hints about neckties, political meetings, yarns, comic songs, anturic salts, nor do the smiles that are situate between a gay corsage and a picture hat. They never wonder, at a loss, what they will do next. Their evenings never drag--are always too short. You may, indeed, catch them at twelve o'clock at night on the flat of their backs; but not in bed! No, in a shed, under a machine, holding a candle (whose paths drop fatness) up to the connecting-rod that is strained, or the wheel that is out of center. They are continually interested, nay, enthralled. They have a machine, and they are perfecting it. They get one part right, and then another goes wrong; and they get that right, and then another goes wrong, and so on. When they are quite sure they have reached perfection, forth issues the machine out of the shed--and in five minutes is smashed up, together with a limb or so of the inventors, just because they had

48

been quite sure too soon. Then the whole business starts again. They do not give up--that particular wreck was, of course, due to a mere oversight; the whole business starts again. For they have glimpsed perfection; they have the gleam of perfection in their souls. Thus their lives run away. 'They will never fly!' you remark, cynically. Well, if they don't? Besides, what about Wright? With all your cynicism, have you never envied them their machine and their passionate interest in it?

You know, perhaps, the moment when, brushing in front of the glass, you detected your first grey hair. You stopped brushing; then you resumed brushing, hastily; you pretended not to be shocked, but you were. Perhaps you know a more disturbing moment than that, the moment when it suddenly occurred to you that you had 'arrived' as far as you ever will arrive; and you had realized as much of your early dream as you ever will realize, and the realization was utterly unlike the dream; the marriage was excessively prosaic and eternal, not at all what you expected it to be; and your illusions were dissipated; and games and hobbies had an unpleasant core of tedium and futility; and the ideal tobacco-mixture did not exist; and one literary masterpiece resembled another; and all the days that are to come will more or less resemble the present day, until you die; and in an illuminating flash you understood what all those people were driving at when they wrote such unconscionably long letters to the _Telegraph_ as to life being worth living or not worth living; and there was naught to be done but face the grey, monotonous future, and pretend to be cheerful with the worm of _ennui_ gnawing at your heart! In a word, the moment when it occurred to you that yours is 'the common lot.' In that moment have you not wished--do you not continually wish--for an exhaustless machine, a machine that you could never get to the end of? Would you not give your head to be lying on the flat of your back, peering with a candle, dirty, foiled, catching cold-- but absorbed in the pursuit of an object? Have you not gloomily regretted that you were born without a mechanical turn, because there is really something about a machine...?

49

It has never struck you that you do possess a machine! Oh, blind! Oh, dull! It has never struck you that you have at hand a machine wonderful beyond all mechanisms in sheds, intricate, delicately adjustable, of astounding and miraculous possibilities, interminably interesting! That machine is yourself. 'This fellow is preaching. I won't have it!' you exclaim resentfully. Dear Sir, I am not preaching, and, even if I were, I think you _would_ have it. I think I can anyhow keep hold of your button for a while, though you pull hard. I am not preaching. I am simply bent on calling your attention to a fact which has perhaps wholly or partially escaped you--namely, that you are the most fascinating bit of machinery that ever was. You do yourself less than justice. It is said that men are only interested in themselves. The truth is that, as a rule, men are interested in every mortal thing except themselves. They have a habit of taking themselves for granted, and that habit is responsible for nine-tenths of the boredom and despair on the face of the planet.

A man will wake up in the middle of the night (usually owing to some form of delightful excess), and his brain will be very active indeed for a space ere he can go to sleep again. In that candid hour, after the exaltation of the evening and before the hope of the dawn, he will see everything in its true colors--except himself. There is nothing like a sleepless couch for a clear vision of one's environment. He will see all his wife's faults and the hopelessness of trying to cure them. He will momentarily see, though with less sharpness of outline, his own faults. He will probably decide that the anxieties of children outweigh the joys connected with children. He will admit all the shortcomings of existence, will face them like a man, grimly, sourly, in a sturdy despair. He will mutter: 'Of course I'm angry! Who wouldn't be? Of course I'm disappointed! Did I expect this twenty years ago? Yes, we ought to save more. But we don't, so there you are! I'm bound to worry! I know I should be better if I didn't smoke so much. I know there's absolutely no sense at all in taking liqueurs. Absurd to be ruffled with her when she's in one of her moods. I don't have enough exercise. Can't be regular, somehow.

Not the slightest use hoping that things will be different, because I know they won't. Queer world! Never really what you may call happy, you know. Now, if things were different ...' He loses consciousness.

Observe: he has taken himself for granted, just glancing at his faults and looking away again. It is his environment that has occupied his attention, and his environment--'things'--that he would wish to have 'different,' did he not know, out of the fullness of experience, that it is futile to desire such a change? What he wants is a pipe that won't put itself into his mouth, a glass that won't leap of its own accord to his lips, money that won't slip untouched out of his pocket, legs that without asking will carry him certain miles every day in the open air, habits that practice themselves, a wife that will expand and contract according to his humors, like a Wernicke bookcase, always complete but never finished. Wise man, he perceives at once that he can't have these things. And so he resigns himself to the universe, and settles down to a permanent, restrained discontent. No one shall say he is unreasonable.

You see, he has given no attention to the machine. Let us not call it a flying-machine. Let us call it simply an automobile. There it is on the road, jolting, screeching, rattling, perfuming. And there he is, saying: 'This road ought to be as smooth as velvet. That hill in front is ridiculous, and the descent on the other side positively dangerous. And it's all turns--I can't see a hundred yards in front.' He has a wild idea of trying to force the County Council to sand-paper the road, or of employing the new Territorial Army to remove the hill. But he dismisses that idea-- he is so reasonable. He accepts all. He sits clothed in reasonableness on the machine, and accepts all. 'Ass!' you exclaim. 'Why doesn't he get down and inflate that tyre, for one thing? Anyone can see the sparking apparatus is wrong, and it's perfectly certain the gear-box wants oil.

Why doesn't he?' I will tell you why he doesn't. Just because he isn't aware that he is on a machine at all. He has never examined what he is on. And at the back of his consciousness is a dim idea that he is perched on a piece of solid, immutable rock that runs on castors.

Chapter II

Amateurs in the Art of Living

Considering that we have to spend the whole of our lives in this human machine, considering that it is our sole means of contact and compromise with the rest of the world, we really do devote to it very little attention. When I say 'we,' I mean our inmost spirits, the instinctive part, the mystery within that exists. And when I say 'the human machine' I mean the brain and the body-- and chiefly the brain. The expression of the soul by means of the brain and body is what we call the art of 'living.' We certainly do not learn this art at school to any appreciable extent. At school we are taught that it is necessary to fling our arms and legs to and fro for so many hours per diem. We are also shown, practically, that our brains are capable of performing certain useful tricks, and that if we do not compel our brains to perform those tricks we shall suffer. Thus one day we run home and proclaim to our delighted parents that eleven twelves are 132. A feat of the brain! So it goes on until our parents begin to look up to us because we can chatter of cosines or sketch the foreign policy of Louis XIV. Good! But not a word about the principles of the art of living yet! Only a few detached rules from our parents, to be blindly followed when particular crises supervene. And, indeed, it would be absurd to talk to a schoolboy about the expression of his soul. He would probably mutter a monosyllable which is not 'mice.'

Of course, school is merely a preparation for living; unless one goes to a university, in which case it is a preparation for university. One is supposed to turn one's attention to living when these preliminaries are over--say at the age of about twenty. Assuredly one lives then; there is, however, nothing new in that, for one has been living all the time, in a fashion; all the time one has been using the machine without understanding it. But does one, school and college being over, enter upon a study of the machine? Not a bit. The question then becomes, not how to live, but how to obtain and retain a position in which one will be able to live; how to get minute portions of dead animals and plants which one can swallow, in order not to die of hunger; how to acquire and constantly renew a stock of other portions of dead animals and plants in which one can envelop oneself in order not to die of cold; how to procure the exclusive right of entry into certain huts where one may sleep and eat without being rained upon by the clouds of heaven. And so forth. And when one has realized this ambition, there comes the desire to be able to double the operation and do it, not for oneself alone, but for oneself and another. Marriage! But no scientific sustained attention is yet given to the real business of living, of smooth intercourse, of self-expression, of conscious adaptation to environment--in brief, to the study of the machine. At thirty the chances are that a man will understand better the draught of a chimney than his own respiratory apparatus--to name one of the simple, obvious things--and as for understanding the working of his own brain--what an idea! As for the skill to avoid the waste of power involved by friction in the business of living, do we give an hour to it in a month? Do we ever at all examine it save in an amateurish and clumsy fashion? A young lady produces a water-color drawing. 'Very nice!' we say, and add, to ourselves, 'For an amateur.' But our living is more amateurish than that young lady's drawing; though surely we ought every one of us to be professionals at living!

When we have been engaged in the preliminaries to living for about fifty-five years, we begin to think about slacking off. Up till this period our reason for not having scientifically studied the art of living--the perfecting and use of the finer parts of the machine--is not that we have lacked leisure (most of us have enormous heaps of leisure), but that we have simply been too absorbed in the preliminaries, have, in fact, treated the preliminaries to the business as the business itself. Then at fifty-five we ought at last to begin to live our lives with professional skill, as a professional painter paints pictures. Yes, but we can't. It is too late then. Neither painters, nor acrobats, nor any professionals can be formed at the age of fifty-five. Thus we finish our lives amateurishly, as we have begun them. And when the machine creaks and sets our teeth on edge, or refuses to obey the steering-wheel and deposits us in the ditch, we say: 'Can't be helped!' or 'Doesn't matter! It will be all the same a hundred years hence!' or: 'I must make the best of things.' And we try to believe that in accepting the _status quo_ we have justified the _status quo_, and all the time we feel our insincerity.

You exclaim that I exaggerate. I do. To force into prominence an aspect of affairs usually overlooked, it is absolutely necessary to exaggerate. Poetic license is one name for this kind of exaggeration. But I exaggerate very little indeed, much less than perhaps you think. I know that you are going to point out to me that vast numbers of people regularly spend a considerable portion of their leisure in striving after self-improvement. Granted! And I am glad of it. But I should be gladder if their strivings bore more closely upon the daily business of living, of self-expression without friction and without futile desires. See this man who regularly studies every evening of his life! He has genuinely understood the nature of poetry, and his taste is admirable. He recites verse with true feeling, and may be said to be highly cultivated. Poetry is a continual source of pleasure to him. True! But why is he always complaining about not receiving his deserts in the office? Why is he worried about finance? Why does he so often sulk with his wife? Why does he persist in eating more than his digestion will tolerate? It was not written in the book of fate that he should complain and worry and sulk and suffer. And if he was a professional at living he would not do these things. There is no reason why he should do

55

them, except the reason that he has never learnt his business, never studied the human machine as a whole, never really thought rationally about living. Supposing you encountered an automobilist who was swerving and grinding all over the road, and you stopped to ask what was the matter, and he replied: 'Never mind what's the matter. Just look at my lovely acetylene lamps, how they shine, and how I've polished them!' You would not regard him as a Clifford-Earp, or even as an entirely sane man. So with our student of poetry. It is indubitable that a large amount of what is known as self-improvement is simply self-indulgence--a form of pleasure which only incidentally improves a particular part of the machine, and even that to the neglect of far more important parts.

My aim is to direct a man's attention to himself as a whole, considered as a machine, complex and capable of quite extraordinary efficiency, for travelling through this world smoothly, in any desired manner, with satisfaction not only to himself but to the people he meets en route, and the people who are overtaking him and whom he is overtaking. My aim is to show that only an inappreciable fraction of our ordered and sustained efforts is given to the business of actual living, as distinguished from the preliminaries to living.

Chapter III

The Brain as a Gentleman-at-large

It is not as if, in this business of daily living, we were seriously hampered by ignorance either as to the results which we ought to obtain, or as to the general means which we must employ in order to obtain them. With all our absorption in the mere preliminaries to living, and all our carelessness about living itself, we arrive pretty soon at a fairly accurate notion of what satisfactory living is, and we perceive with some clearness the methods necessary to success. I have pictured the man who wakes up in the middle of the night and sees the horrid semi-fiasco of his life. But let me picture the man who wakes up refreshed early on a fine summer morning and looks into his mind with the eyes of hope and experience, not experience and despair. That man will pass a delightful half-hour in thinking upon the scheme of the universe as it affects himself. He is quite clear that contentment depends on his own acts, and that no power can prevent him from performing those acts. He plans everything out, and before he gets up he knows precisely what he must and will do in certain foreseen crises and junctures. He sincerely desires to live efficiently--who would wish to make a daily mess of existence?--and he knows the way to realize the desire.

And yet, mark me! That man will not have been an hour on his feet on this difficult earth before the machine has unmistakably gone wrong: the machine which was designed to do this work of living, which is capable of doing it thoroughly well, but which has not been put into order! What is the use of consulting the map of life and tracing the itinerary, and getting the machine out of the shed, and making a start, if half the nuts are loose, or the steering pillar is twisted, or there is no petrol in the tank? (Having asked this question, I will drop the mechanical-vehicular comparison, which is too rough and crude for the delicacy of the subject.) Where has the human machine gone wrong? It has gone wrong in the brain. What, is he 'wrong in the head'? Most assuredly, most strictly. He knows--none better--that when his wife employs a particular tone containing ten grains of asperity, and he replies in a particular tone containing eleven grains, the consequences will be explosive. He knows, on the other hand, that if he replies in a tone containing only one little drop of honey, the consequences may not be unworthy of two reasonable beings. He knows this. His brain is fully instructed. And lo! his brain, while arguing that women are really too absurd (as if that was the point), is sending down orders to the muscles of the throat and mouth which result in at least eleven grains of asperity, and conjugal relations are endangered for the day. He didn't want to do it. His desire was not to do it. He despises himself for doing it. But his brain was not in working order. His brain ran away--'raced'--on its own account, against reason, against desire, against morning resolves--and there he is!

That is just one example, of the simplest and slightest. Examples can be multiplied. The man may be a young man whose immediate future depends on his passing an examination--an examination which he is capable of passing 'on his head,' which nothing can prevent him from passing if only his brain will not be so absurd as to give orders to his legs to walk out of the house towards the tennis court instead of sending them upstairs to the study; if only, having once safely lodged him in the study, his brain will devote itself to the pages of books instead of dwelling on the image of a nice girl--not at all like other girls. Or the man may be an old man who will live in perfect comfort if only his brain will not interminably run round and round in a circle of grievances, apprehensions, and fears which no amount of contemplation can destroy or even ameliorate.

The brain, the brain--that is the seat of trouble! 'Well,' you say, 'of course it is. We all know that!' We don't act as if we did, anyway. 'Give us more brains, Lord!' ejaculated a great writer. Personally, I think he would have been wiser if he had asked first for the power to keep in order such brains as we have. We indubitably possess quite enough brains, quite as much as we can handle. The supreme muddlers of living are often people of quite remarkable intellectual faculty, with a quite remarkable gift of being wise for others. The pity is that our brains have a way of 'wandering,' as it is politely called. Brain-wandering is indeed now recognized as a specific disease. I wonder what you, O business man with an office in Ludgate Circus, would say to your office-boy, whom you had dispatched on an urgent message to Westminster, and whom you found larking around Euston Station when you rushed to catch your week-end train. 'Please, sir, I started to go to Westminster, but there's something funny in my limbs that makes me go up all manner of streets. I can't help it, sir!' 'Can't you?' you would say. 'Well, you had better go and be somebody else's office-boy.' Your brain is something worse than that office-boy, something more insidiously potent for evil.

I conceive the brain of the average well-intentioned man as possessing the tricks and manners of one of those gentlemen-at-large who, having nothing very urgent to do, stroll along and offer their services gratis to some shorthanded work of philanthropy. They will commonly demoralize and disorganize the business conduct of an affair in about a fortnight. They come when they like; they go when they like. Sometimes they are exceedingly industrious and obedient, but then there is an even chance that they will shirk and follow their own sweet will. And they mustn't be spoken to, or pulled up--for have they not kindly volunteered, and are they not giving their days for naught!

59

These persons are the bane of the enterprises in which they condescend to meddle. Now, there is a vast deal too much of the gentleman-at-large about one's brain. One's brain has no right whatever to behave as a gentleman-at-large: but it in fact does. It forgets; it flatly ignores orders; at the critical moment when pressure is highest, it simply lights a cigarette and goes out for a walk. And we meekly sit down under this behavior! 'I didn't feel like stewing,' says the young man who, against his wish, will fail in his examination. 'The words were out of my mouth before I knew it,' says the husband whose wife is a woman. 'I couldn't get any inspiration to-day,' says the artist. 'I can't resist Stilton,' says the fellow who is dying of greed. 'One can't help one's thoughts,' says the old worrier. And this last really voices the secret excuse of all five.

And you all say to me: 'My brain is myself. How can I alter myself? I was born like that.' In the first place you were not born 'like that,' you have lapsed to that. And in the second place your brain is not yourself. It is only a part of yourself, and not the highest seat of authority. Do you love your mother, wife, or children with your brain? Do you desire with your brain? Do you, in a word, ultimately and essentially "live" with your brain? No. Your brain is an instrument. The proof that it is an instrument lies in the fact that, when extreme necessity urges, you can command your brain to do certain things, and it does them. The first of the two great principles which underlie the efficiency of the human machine is this: *The brain is a servant, exterior to the central force of the Ego.* If it is out of control the reason is not that it is uncontrollable, but merely that its discipline has been neglected. The brain can be trained, as the hand and eye can be trained; it can be made as obedient as a sporting dog, and by similar methods. In the meantime the indispensable preparation for brain discipline is to form the habit of regarding one's brain as an instrument exterior to one's self, like a tongue or a foot.

Chapter IV

The First Practical Step

The brain is a highly quaint organism. Let me say at once, lest I should be cannonaded by physiologists, psychologists, or metaphysicians, that by the 'brain' I mean the faculty which reasons and which gives orders to the muscles. I mean exactly what the plain man means by the brain. The brain is the diplomatist which arranges relations between our instinctive self and the universe, and it fulfils its mission when it provides for the maximum of freedom to the instincts with the minimum of friction. It argues with the instincts. It takes them on one side and points out the non-wisdom of certain performances. It catches them by the coat-tails when they are about to make fools of themselves. 'Don't drink all that iced champagne at a draught,' it says to one instinct; 'we may die of it.' 'Don't catch that rude fellow one in the eye,' it says to another instinct; 'he is more powerful than us.' It is, in fact, a majestic spectacle of common sense. And yet it has the most extraordinary lapses. It is just like that man--we all know him and consult him--who is a continual fount of excellent, sagacious advice on everything, but who somehow cannot bring his sagacity to bear on his own personal career.

In the matter of its own special activities the brain is usually undisciplined and unreliable. We never know what it will do next. We give it some work to do, say, as we are walking along the street to the office. Perhaps it has to devise some scheme for making L150 suffice for L200, or perhaps it has to plan out the heads of a very important letter. We meet a pretty woman, and away that undisciplined, sagacious brain runs after her, dropping the scheme or the draft letter, and amusing itself with aspirations or regrets for half an hour, an hour, sometimes a day. The serious part of our instinctive self feebly remonstrates, but without effect. Or it may be that we have suffered a great disappointment, which is definite and hopeless. Will the brain, like a sensible creature, leave that disappointment alone, and instead of living in the past live in the present or the future? Not it! Though it knows perfectly well that it is wasting its time and casting a very painful and utterly unnecessary gloom over itself and us, it can so little control its unhealthy morbid appetite that no expostulations will induce it to behave rationally. Or perhaps, after a confabulation with the soul, it has been decided that when next a certain harmful instinct comes into play the brain shall firmly interfere. 'Yes,' says the brain, 'I really will watch that.' But when the moment arrives, is the brain on the spot? The brain has probably forgotten the affair entirely, or remembered it too late; or sighs, as the victorious instinct knocks it on the head: 'Well, next time!'

All this, and much more that every reader can supply from his own exciting souvenirs, is absurd and ridiculous on the part of the brain. It is a conclusive proof that the brain is out of condition, idle as a nigger, capricious as an actor-manager, and eaten to the core with loose habits. Therefore the brain must be put into training. It is the most important part of the human machine by which the soul expresses and develops itself, and it must learn good habits. And primarily it must be taught obedience. Obedience can only be taught by imposing one's will, by the sheer force of volition. And the brain must be mastered by will-power. The beginning of wise living lies in the control of the brain by the will; so that the brain may act according to the precepts which the brain itself gives. With an obedient disciplined brain a man may live always right up to the standard of his best moments.

To teach a child obedience you tell it to do something, and you see that that something is done. The same with the brain. Here is the foundation of an efficient life and the antidote for the tendency to make a fool of oneself. It is marvelously simple. Say to your brain: 'From 9 o'clock to 9.30 this morning you must dwell without ceasing on a particular topic which I will give you.' Now, it doesn't matter what this topic is--the point is to control and invigorate the brain by exercise--but you may just as well give it a useful topic to think over as a futile one. You might give it this: 'My brain is my servant. I am not the play-thing of my brain.' Let it concentrate on these statements for thirty minutes. 'What?' you cry. 'Is this the way to an efficient life? Why, there's nothing in it!' Simple as it may appear, this _is_ the way, and it is the only way. As for there being nothing in it, try it. I guarantee that you will fail to keep your brain concentrated on the given idea for thirty seconds--let alone thirty minutes. You will find your brain conducting itself in a manner which would be comic were it not tragic. Your first experiments will result in disheartening failure, for to exact from the brain, at will and by will, concentration on a given idea for even so short a period as half an hour is an exceedingly difficult feat--and a fatiguing! It needs perseverance. It needs a terrible obstinacy on the part of the will. That brain of yours will be hopping about all over the place, and every time it hops you must bring it back by force to its original position. You must absolutely compel it to ignore every idea except the one which you have selected for its attention. You cannot hope to triumph all at once. But you can hope to triumph. There is no royal road to the control of the brain. There is no patent dodge about it, and no complicated function which a plain person may not comprehend. It is simply a question of: 'I will, I will, and I will.'

Let me resume. Efficient living, living up to one's best standard, getting the last ounce of power out of the machine with the minimum of friction: these things depend on the disciplined and vigorous condition of the brain. The brain can be disciplined by learning the habit of obedience. And it can learn the habit of obedience by the practice of concentration. Disciplinary concentration, though nothing could have the air of being simpler, is the basis of the whole structure. This fact must be grasped imaginatively; it must be seen and felt. The more regularly concentration is practiced, the more firmly will the imagination grasp the effects of it, both direct and indirect. After but a few days of honest trying in the exercise which I have indicated, you will perceive its influence. You will grow accustomed to the idea, at first strange in its novelty, of the brain being external to the supreme force which is _you_, and in subjection to that force. You will, as a not very distant possibility, see yourself in possession of the power to switch your brain on and off in a particular subject as you switch electricity on and off in a particular room. The brain will get used to the straight paths of obedience. And--a remarkable phenomenon--it will, by the mere practice of obedience, become less forgetful and more effective. It will not so frequently give way to an instinct that takes it by surprise. In a word, it will have received a general tonic. With a brain that is improving every day you can set about the perfecting of the machine in a scientific manner.

Chapter V

Habit-forming by Concentration

As soon as the will has got the upper hand of the brain--as soon as it can say to the brain, with a fair certainty of being obeyed: 'Do this. Think along these lines, and continue to do so without wandering until I give you leave to stop'--then is the time arrived when the perfecting of the human machine may be undertaken in a large and comprehensive spirit, as a city council undertakes the purification and reconstruction of a city. The tremendous possibilities of an obedient brain will be perceived immediately we begin to reflect upon what we mean by our 'character.' Now, a person's character is, and can be, nothing else but the total result of his habits of thought. A person is benevolent because he habitually thinks benevolently. A person is idle because his thoughts dwell habitually on the instant pleasures of idleness. It is true that everybody is born with certain predispositions, and that these predispositions influence very strongly the early formation of habits of thought. But the fact remains that the character is built by long-continued habits of thought. If the mature edifice of character usually shows in an exaggerated form the peculiarities of the original predisposition, this merely indicates a probability that the slow erection of the edifice has proceeded at haphazard, and that reason has not presided over it. A child may be born with a tendency to bent shoulders. If nothing is done, if on the contrary he becomes a clerk and abhors gymnastics, his shoulders will develop an excessive roundness, entirely through habit. Whereas, if his will, guided by his reason, had compelled the formation of a

65

corrective physical habit, his shoulders might have been, if not quite straight, nearly so. Thus a physical habit! The same with a mental habit.

The more closely we examine the development of original predispositions, the more clearly we shall see that this development is not inevitable, is not a process which works itself out independently according to mysterious, ruthless laws which we cannot understand. For instance, the effect of an original predisposition may be destroyed by an accidental shock. A young man with an inherited tendency to alcohol may develop into a stern teetotaler through the shock caused by seeing his drunken father strike his mother; whereas, if his father had chanced to be affectionate in drink, the son might have ended in the gutter. No ruthless law here! It is notorious, also, that natures are sometimes completely changed in their development by chance momentary contact with natures stronger than themselves. 'From that day I resolved--' etc. You know the phrase. Often the resolve is not kept; but often it is kept. A spark has inflamed the will. The burning will has tyrannized over the brain. New habits have been formed. And the result looks just like a miracle.

Now, if these great transformations can be brought about by accident, cannot similar transformations be brought about by a reasonable design? At any rate, if one starts to bring them about, one starts with the assurance that transformations are not impossible, since they have occurred. One starts also in the full knowledge of the influence of habit on life. Take any one of your own habits, mental or physical. You will be able to recall the time when that habit did not exist, or if it did exist it was scarcely perceptible. And you will discover that nearly all your habits have been formed unconsciously, by daily repetitions which bore no relation to a general plan, and which you practiced not noticing. You will be compelled to admit that your 'character,' as it is to-day, is a structure that has been built almost without the aid of an architect; higgledy-piggledy, anyhow. But occasionally the architect did step in and design something. Here and there among your habits you will find one that you consciously and of deliberate purpose initiated and persevered with--doubtless owing to some happy influence. What is the difference between that conscious habit and the unconscious habits? None whatever as regards its effect on the sum of your character. It may be the strongest of all your habits. The only quality that differentiates it from the others is that it has a definite object (most likely a good object), and that it wholly or partially fulfils that object. There is not a man who reads these lines but has, in this detail or that, proved in himself that the will, forcing the brain to repeat the same action again and again, can modify the shape of his character as a sculptor modifies the shape of damp clay.

But if a grown man's character is developing from day to day (as it is), if nine-tenths of the development is due to unconscious action and one-tenth to conscious action, and if the one-tenth conscious is the most satisfactory part of the total result; why, in the name of common sense, henceforward, should not nine-tenths, instead of one-tenth, be due to conscious action? What is there to prevent this agreeable consummation? There is nothing whatever to prevent it--except insubordination on the part of the brain. And insubordination of the brain can be cured, as I have previously shown. When I see men unhappy and inefficient in the craft of _living_, from sheer, crass inattention to their own development; when I see misshapen men building up businesses and empires, and never stopping to build up themselves; when I see dreary men expending precisely the same energy on teaching a dog to walk on its hind-legs as would brighten the whole color of their own lives, I feel as if I wanted to give up the ghost, so ridiculous, so fatuous does the spectacle seem! But, of course, I do not give up the ghost. The paroxysm passes. Only I really must cry out: 'Can't you see what you're missing? Can't you see that you're missing the most interesting thing on earth, far more interesting than businesses, empires, and dogs? Doesn't it strike you how clumsy and short-sighted you are--working always with

67

an inferior machine when you might have a smooth-gliding perfection? Doesn't it strike you how badly you are treating yourself?'

Listen, you confirmed grumbler, you who make the evening meal hideous with complaints against destiny--for it is you I will single out. Are you aware what people are saying about you behind your back? They are saying that you render yourself and your family miserable by the habit which has grown on you of always grumbling. 'Surely it isn't as bad as that?' you protest. Yes, it is just as bad as that. You say: 'The fact is, I know it's absurd to grumble. But I'm like that. I've tried to stop it, and I can't!' How have you tried to stop it? 'Well, I've made up my mind several times to fight against it, but I never succeed. This is strictly between ourselves. I don't usually admit that I'm a grumbler.' Considering that you grumble for about an hour and a half every day of your life, it was sanguine, my dear sir, to expect to cure such a habit by means of a solitary intention, formed at intervals in the brain and then forgotten. No! You must do more than that. If you will daily fix your brain firmly for half an hour on the truth (you know it to be a truth) that grumbling is absurd and futile, your brain will henceforward begin to form a habit in that direction; it will begin to be molded to the idea that grumbling is absurd and futile. In odd moments, when it isn't thinking of anything in particular, it will suddenly remember that grumbling is absurd and futile. When you sit down to the meal and open your mouth to say: 'I can't think what my ass of a partner means by--' it will remember that grumbling is absurd and futile, and will alter the arrangement of your throat, teeth, and tongue, so that you will say: 'What fine weather we're having!' In brief, it will remember involuntarily, by a new habit. All who look into their experience will admit that the failure to replace old habits by new ones is due to the fact that at the critical moment the brain does not remember; it simply forgets. The practice of concentration will cure that. All depends on regular concentration. This grumbling is an instance, though chosen not quite at hazard.

68

Chapter VI

Lord Over the Noddle

Having proved by personal experiment the truth of the first of the two great principles which concern the human machine-- namely, that the brain is a servant, not a master, and can be controlled--we may now come to the second. The second is more fundamental than the first, but it can be of no use until the first is understood and put into practice. The human machine is an apparatus of brain and muscle for enabling the Ego to develop freely in the universe by which it is surrounded, without friction. Its function is to convert the facts of the universe to the best advantage of the Ego. The facts of the universe are the material with which it is its business to deal--not the facts of an ideal universe, but the facts of this universe. Hence, when friction occurs, when the facts of the universe cease to be of advantage to the Ego, the fault is in the machine. It is not the solar system that has gone wrong, but the human machine. Second great principle, therefore: 'In case of friction, the machine is always at fault.'

You can control nothing but your own mind. Even your two-year-old babe may defy you by the instinctive force of its personality. But your own mind you can control. Your own mind is a sacred enclosure into which nothing harmful can enter except by your permission. Your own mind has the power to transmute every external phenomenon to its own purposes. If happiness arises from cheerfulness, kindliness, and rectitude (and who will deny it?), what possible combination of

69

circumstances is going to make you unhappy so long as the machine remains in order? If self-development consists in the utilization of one's environment (not utilization of somebody else's environment), how can your environment prevent you from developing? You would look rather foolish without it, anyway. In that noddle of yours is everything necessary for development, for the maintaining of dignity, for the achieving of happiness, and you are absolute lord over the noddle, will you but exercise the powers of lordship. Why worry about the contents of somebody else's noddle, in which you can be nothing but an intruder, when you may arrive at a better result, with absolute certainty, by confining your activities to your own? 'Look within.' 'The Kingdom of Heaven is within you.' 'Oh, yes!' you protest. 'All that's old. Epictetus said that. Marcus Aurelius said that. Christ said that.' They did. I admit it readily. But if you were ruffled this morning because your motor-omnibus broke down, and you had to take a cab, then so far as you are concerned these great teachers lived in vain. You, calling yourself a reasonable man, are going about dependent for your happiness, dignity, and growth, upon a thousand things over which you have no control, and the most exquisitely organized machine for ensuring happiness, dignity, and growth, is rusting away inside you. And all because you have a sort of notion that a saying said two thousand years ago cannot be practical.

You remark sagely to your child: 'No, my child, you cannot have that moon, and you will accomplish nothing by crying for it. Now, here is this beautiful box of bricks, by means of which you may amuse yourself while learning many wonderful matters and improving your mind. You must try to be content with what you have, and to make the best of it. If you had the moon you wouldn't be any happier.' Then you lie awake half the night repining because the last post has brought a letter to the effect that 'the Board cannot entertain your application for,' etc. You say the two cases are not alike. They are not. Your child has never heard of Epictetus. On the other hand, justice is the moon. At your age you surely know that. 'But the Directors ought to have granted my application,' you insist. Exactly! I agree. But we are not in a universe of "oughts." You have a special apparatus within you for dealing with a universe where "oughts" are flagrantly disregarded. And you are not using it. You are lying awake, keeping your wife awake, injuring your health, injuring hers, losing your dignity and your cheerfulness. Why? Because you think that these antics and performances will influence the Board? Because you think that they will put you into a better condition for dealing with your environment to-morrow? Not a bit. Simply because the machine is at fault.

In certain cases we do make use of our machines (as well as their sad condition of neglect will allow), but in other cases we behave in an extraordinarily irrational manner. Thus if we sally out and get caught in a heavy shower we do not, unless very far gone in foolishness, sit down and curse the weather. We put up our umbrella, if we have one, and if not we hurry home. We may grumble, but it is not serious grumbling; we accept the shower as a fact of the universe, and control ourselves. Thus also, if by a sudden catastrophe we lose somebody who is important to us, we grieve, but we control ourselves, recognizing one of those hazards of destiny from which not even millionaires are exempt. And the result on our Ego is usually to improve it in essential respects. But there are other strokes of destiny, other facts of the universe, against which we protest as a child protests when deprived of the moon.

Take the case of an individual with an imperfect idea of honesty. Now, that individual is the consequence of his father and mother and his environment, and his father and mother of theirs, and so backwards to the single-celled protoplasm. That individual is a result of the cosmic order, the inevitable product of cause and effect. We know that. We must admit that he is just as much a fact of the universe as a shower of rain or a storm at sea that swallows a ship. We freely grant in the abstract that there must be, at the present stage of evolution, a certain number of persons with unfair minds. We are quite ready to contemplate

71

such an individual with philosophy--until it happens that, in the course of the progress of the solar system, he runs up against ourselves. Then listen to the outcry! Listen to the continual explosions of a righteous man aggrieved! The individual may be our clerk, cashier, son, father, brother, partner, wife, employer. We are ill-used! We are being treated unfairly! We kick; we scream. We nourish the inward sense of grievance that eats the core out of content. We sit down in the rain. We decline to think of umbrellas, or to run to shelter.

We care not that that individual is a fact which the universe has been slowly manufacturing for millions of years. Our attitude implies that we want eternity to roll back and begin again, in such wise that we at any rate shall not be disturbed. Though we have a machine for the transmutation of facts into food for our growth, we do not dream of using it. But, we say, he is doing us harm! Where? In our minds. He has robbed us of our peace, our comfort, our happiness, our good temper. Even if he has, we might just as well inveigh against a shower. But has he? What was our brain doing while this naughty person stepped in and robbed us of the only possessions worth having? No, no! It is not that he has done us harm--the one cheerful item in a universe of stony facts is that no one can harm anybody except himself--it is merely that we have been silly, precisely as silly as if we had taken a seat in the rain with a folded umbrella by our side.... The machine is at fault. I fancy we are now obtaining glimpses of what that phrase really means.

Chapter VII

What 'Living' Chiefly Is

Keep The PEACE, NOTHING BuT The PEACE w/ OTHERS

It is in intercourse--social, sentimental, or business--with one's
fellows that the qualities and the condition of the human
machine are put to the test and strained. That part of my life
which I conduct by myself, without reference--or at any rate
without direct reference--to others, I can usually manage in such
a way that the gods do not positively weep at the spectacle
thereof. My environment is simpler, less puzzling, when I am
alone, my calm and my self-control less liable to violent
fluctuations. Impossible to be disturbed by a chair! Impossible
that a chair should get on one's nerves! Impossible to blame a
chair for not being as reasonable, as archangelic as I am myself!
But when it comes to people! Well, that is 'living,' then! The art
of life, the art of extracting all its power from the human
machine, does not lie chiefly in processes of bookish-culture, nor
in contemplations of the beauty and majesty of existence. It lies
chiefly in keeping the peace, the whole peace, and nothing but
the peace, with those with whom one is 'thrown.' Is it in sitting
ecstatic over Shelley, Shakespeare, or Herbert Spencer, solitary
in my room of a night, that I am 'improving myself' and learning
to live? Or is it in watching over all my daily human contacts?
Do not seek to escape the comparison by insinuating that I
despise study, or by pointing out that the eternal verities are
beyond dailiness. Nothing of the kind! I am so 'silly' about books
that merely to possess them gives me pleasure. And if the
verities are good for eternity they ought to be good for a day. If I
cannot exchange them for daily coin--if I can't buy happiness for
a single day because I've nothing less than an eternal verity

about me and nobody has sufficient change--then my eternal verity is not an eternal verity. It is merely an unnegotiable bit of glass (called a diamond), or even a note on the Bank of Engraving.

I can say to myself when I arise in the morning: 'I am master of my brain. No one can get in there and rage about like a bull in a china shop. If my companions on the planet's crust choose to rage about they cannot affect me! I will not let them. I have power to maintain my own calm, and I will. No earthly being can force me to be false to my principles, or to be blind to the beauty of the universe, or to be gloomy, or to be irritable, or to complain against my lot. For these things depend on the brain; cheerfulness, kindliness, and honest thinking are all within the department of the brain. The disciplined brain can accomplish them. And my brain is disciplined, and I will discipline it more and more as the days pass. I am, therefore, independent of hazard, and I will back myself to conduct all intercourse as becomes a rational creature.' I can say this. I can ram this argument by force of will into my brain, and by dint of repeating it often enough I shall assuredly arrive at the supreme virtues of reason. I should assuredly conquer--the brain being such a machine of habit--even if I did not take the trouble to consider in the slightest degree what manner of things my fellow-men are--by acting merely in my own interests. But the way of perfection (I speak relatively) will be immensely shortened and smoothed if I do consider, dispassionately, the case of the other human machines. Thus:--

The truth is that my attitude towards my fellows is fundamentally and totally wrong, and that it entails on my thinking machine a strain which is quite unnecessary, though I may have arranged the machine so as to withstand the strain successfully. The secret of smooth living is a calm cheerfulness which will leave me always in full possession of my reasoning faculty--in order that I may live by reason instead of by instinct and momentary passion. The secret of calm cheerfulness is

74

kindliness; no person can be consistently cheerful and calm who does not consistently think kind thoughts. But how can I be kindly when I pass the major portion of my time in blaming the people who surround me--who are part of my environment? If I, blaming, achieve some approach to kindliness, it is only by a great and exhausting effort of self-mastery. The inmost secret, then, lies in not blaming, in not judging and emitting verdicts. Oh! I do not blame by word of mouth! I am far too advanced for such a puerility. I keep the blame in my own breast, where it festers. I am always privately forgiving, which is bad for me. Because, you know, there is nothing to forgive. I do not have to forgive bad weather; nor, if I found myself in an earthquake, should I have to forgive the earthquake.

All blame, uttered or unexpressed, is wrong. I do not blame myself. I can explain myself to myself. I can invariably explain myself. If I forged a friend's name on a check I should explain the affair quite satisfactorily to myself. And instead of blaming myself I should sympathize with myself for having been driven into such an excessively awkward corner. Let me examine honestly my mental processes, and I must admit that my attitude towards others is entirely different from my attitude towards myself. I must admit that in the seclusion of my mind, though I say not a word, I am constantly blaming others because I am not happy. Whenever I bump up against an opposing personality and my smooth progress is impeded, I secretly blame the opposer. I act as though I had shouted to the world: 'Clear out of the way, every one, for I am coming!' Everyone does not clear out of the way. I did not really expect everyone to clear out of the way. But I act, within, as though I had so expected. I blame. Hence kindliness, hence cheerfulness, is rendered vastly more difficult for me.

What I ought to do is this! I ought to reflect again and again, and yet again, that the beings among whom I have to steer, the living environment out of which I have to manufacture my happiness, are just as inevitable in the scheme of evolution as I am myself;

have just as much right to be themselves as I have to be myself; are precisely my equals in the face of Nature; are capable of being explained as I am capable of being explained; are entitled to the same latitude as I am entitled to, and are no more responsible for their composition and their environment than I for mine. I ought to reflect again and again, and yet again, that they all deserve from me as much sympathy as I give to myself. Why not? Having thus reflected in a general manner, I ought to take one by one the individuals with whom I am brought into frequent contact, and seek, by a deliberate effort of the imagination and the reason, to understand them, to understand why they act thus and thus, what their difficulties are, what their 'explanation' is, and how friction can be avoided. So I ought to reflect, morning after morning, until my brain is saturated with the cases of these individuals. Here is a course of discipline. If I follow it I shall gradually lose the preposterous habit of blaming, and I shall have laid the foundations of that quiet, unshakable self-possession which is the indispensable preliminary of conduct according to reason, of thorough efficiency in the machine of happiness. But something in me, something distinctly base, says: 'Yes. The put-yourself-in-his-place business over again! The do-unto-others business over again!' Just so! Something in me is ashamed of being 'moral.' (You all know the feeling!) Well, morals are naught but another name for reasonable conduct; a higher and more practical form of egotism--an egotism which, while freeing others, frees myself. I have tried the lower form of egotism. And it has failed. If I am afraid of being moral, if I prefer to cut off my nose to spite my face, well, I must accept the consequences. But truth will prevail.

Chapter VIII

The Daily Friction

It is with common daily affairs that I am now dealing, not with heroic enterprises, ambitions, martyrdoms. Take the day, the ordinary day in the ordinary house or office. Though it comes seven times a week, and is the most banal thing imaginable, it is quite worth attention. How does the machine get through it? Ah! The best that can be said of the machine is that it does get through it, somehow. The friction, though seldom such as to bring matters to a standstill, is frequent--the sort of friction that, when it occurs in a bicycle, is just sufficient to annoy the rider, but not sufficient to make him get off the machine and examine the bearings. Occasionally the friction is very loud; indeed, disturbing, and at rarer intervals it shrieks, like an omnibus brake out of order. You know those days when you have the sensation that life is not large enough to contain the household or the office-staff, when the business of intercourse may be compared to the maneuvers of two people who, having awakened with a bad headache, are obliged to dress simultaneously in a very small bedroom. 'After you with that towel!' in accents of bitter, grinding politeness. 'If you could kindly move your things off this chair!' in a voice that would blow brains out if it were a bullet. I venture to say that you know those days. 'But,' you reply, 'such days are few. Usually...!' Well, usually, the friction, though less intense, is still proceeding. We grow accustomed to it. We scarcely notice it, as a person in a stuffy chamber will scarcely notice the stuffiness. But the deteriorating influence due to friction goes on, even if unperceived. And one morning we perceive its ravages--and write a letter to the "Telegraph" to inquire whether life is worth living, or whether marriage is a failure, or whether men are more polite than women. The proof that friction, in various and varying degrees, is practically conscious in most households lies in the fact that when we chance on a household where there is no friction we are startled. We can't recover from the phenomenon. And in describing this household to our friends, we say: 'They get on so well together,' as if we were saying: 'They have wings and can fly! Just fancy! Did you ever hear of such a thing?'

Ninety per cent of all daily friction is caused by tone--mere tone of voice. Try this experiment. Say: 'Oh, you little darling, you sweet pet, you entirely charming creature!' to a baby or a dog; but roar these delightful epithets in the tone of saying: 'You infernal little nuisance! If I hear another sound I'll break every bone in your body!' The baby will infallibly whimper, and the dog will infallibly mouch off. True, a dog is not a human being, neither is a baby. They cannot understand. It is precisely because they cannot understand and articulate words that the experiment is valuable; for it separates the effect of the tone from the effect of the word spoken. He who speaks, speaks twice. His words convey his thought, and his tone conveys his mental attitude towards the person spoken to. And certainly the attitude, so far as friction goes, is more important than the thought. Your wife may say to you: 'I shall buy that hat I spoke to you about.' And you may reply, quite sincerely, 'As you please.' But it will depend on your tone whether you convey: 'As you please. I am sympathetically anxious that your innocent caprices should be indulged.' Or whether you convey: 'As you please. Only don't bother me with hats. I am above hats. A great deal too much money is spent in this house on hats. However, I'm helpless!' Or whether you convey: 'As you please, heart of my heart, but if you would like to be a nice girl, go gently. We're

78

rather tight.' I need not elaborate. I am sure of being comprehended.

As tone is the expression of attitude, it is, of course, caused by attitude. The frictional tone is chiefly due to that general attitude of blame which I have already condemned as being absurd and unjustifiable. As, by constant watchful discipline, we gradually lose this silly attitude of blame, so the tone will of itself gradually change. But the two ameliorations can proceed together, and it is a curious thing that an agreeable tone, artificially and deliberately adopted, will influence the mental attitude almost as much as the mental attitude will influence the tone. If you honestly feel resentful against someone, but, having understood the foolishness of fury, intentionally mask your fury under a persuasive tone, your fury will at once begin to abate. You will be led into a rational train of thought; you will see that after all the object of your resentment has a right to exist, and that he is neither a doormat nor a scoundrel, and that anyhow nothing is to be gained, and much is to be lost, by fury. You will see that fury is unworthy of you.

Do you remember the gentleness of the tone which you employed after the healing of your first quarrel with a beloved companion? Do you remember the persuasive tone which you used when you wanted to obtain something from a difficult person on whom your happiness depended? Why should not your tone always combine these qualities? Why should you not carefully school your tone? Is it beneath you to ensure the largest possible amount of your own 'way' by the simplest means? Or is there at the back of your mind that peculiarly English and German idea that politeness, sympathy, and respect for another immortal soul would imply deplorable weakness on your part? You say that your happiness does not depend on every person whom you happen to speak to. Yes, it does. Your happiness is always dependent on just that person. Produce friction, and you suffer. Idle to argue that the person has no business to be upset by your tone! You have caused avoidable

79

friction, simply because your machine for dealing with your environment was suffering from pride, ignorance, or thoughtlessness. You say I am making a mountain out of a mole-hill. No! I am making a mountain out of ten million mole-hills. And that is what life does. It is the little but continuous causes that have great effects. I repeat: Why not deliberately adopt a gentle, persuasive tone--just to see what the results are? Surely you are not ashamed to be wise. You may smile superiorly as you read this. Yet you know very well that more than once you _have_ resolved to use a gentle and persuasive tone on all occasions, and that the sole reason why you had that fearful shindy yesterday with your cousin's sister-in-law was that you had long since failed to keep your resolve. But you were of my mind once, and more than once.

What you have to do is to teach the new habit to your brain by daily concentration on it; by forcing your brain to think of nothing else for half an hour of a morning. After a time the brain will begin to remember automatically. For, of course, the explanation of your previous failures is that your brain, undisciplined, merely forgot at the critical moment. The tone was out of your mouth before your brain had waked up. It is necessary to watch, as though you were a sentinel, not only against the wrong tone, but against the other symptoms of the attitude of blame. Such as the frown. It is necessary to regard yourself constantly, and in minute detail. You lie in bed for half an hour and enthusiastically concentrate on this beautiful new scheme of the right tone. You rise, and because you don't achieve a proper elegance of necktie at the first knotting, you frown and swear and clench your teeth! There is a symptom of the wrong attitude towards your environment. You are awake, but your brain isn't. It is in such a symptom that you may judge yourself. And not a trifling symptom either! If you will frown at a necktie, if you will use language to a necktie which no gentleman should use to a necktie, what will you be capable of to a responsible being?... Yes, it is very difficult. But it can be done.

Chapter IX

'Fire!'

In this business of daily living, of ordinary usage of the machine in hourly intercourse, there occurs sometimes a phenomenon which is the cause of a great deal of trouble, and the result of a very ill-tended machine. It is a phenomenon impossible to ignore, and yet, so shameful is it, so degrading, so shocking, so miserable, that I hesitate to mention it. For one class of reader is certain to ridicule me, loftily saying: 'One really doesn't expect to find this sort of thing in print nowadays!' And another class of reader is certain to get angry. Nevertheless, as one of my main objects in the present book is to discuss matters which 'people don't talk about,' I shall discuss this matter. But my diffidence in doing so is such that I must approach it deviously, describing it first by means of a figure.

Imagine that, looking at a man's house, you suddenly perceive it to be on fire. The flame is scarcely perceptible. You could put it out if you had a free hand. But you have not got a free hand. It is his house, not yours. He may or may not know that his house is burning. You are aware, by experience, however, that if you directed his attention to the flame, the effect of your warning would be exceedingly singular, almost incredible. For the effect would be that he would instantly begin to strike matches, pour on petroleum, and fan the flame, violently resenting interference. Therefore you can only stand and watch, hoping that he will notice the flames before they are beyond control, and extinguish them. The probability is, however, that he will notice the flames too late. And powerless to avert disaster, you are condemned, therefore, to watch the damage of valuable property. The flames leap higher and higher, and they do not die down till they have burned themselves out. You avert your gaze from the spectacle, and until you are gone the owner of the house pretends that nothing has occurred. When alone he curses himself for his carelessness.

The foregoing is meant to be a description of what happens when a man passes through the incendiary experience known as 'losing his temper.' (There! the cat of my chapter is out of the bag!) A man who has lost his temper is simply being 'burnt out.' His constitutes one of the most curious and (for everybody) humiliating spectacles that life offers. It is an insurrection, a boiling over, a sweeping storm. Dignity, common sense, justice are shriveled up and destroyed. Anarchy reigns. The devil has broken his chain. Instinct is stamping on the face of reason. And in that man civilization has temporarily receded millions of years. Of course, the thing amounts to a nervous disease, and I think it is almost universal. You at once protest that you never lose your temper--haven't lost your temper for ages! But do you not mean that you have not smashed furniture for ages? These fires are of varying intensities. Some of them burn very dully. Yet they burn. One man loses his temper; another is merely 'ruffled.' But the event is the same in kind. When you are 'ruffled,' when you are conscious of a resentful vibration that surprises all your being, when your voice changes, when you notice a change in the demeanor of your companion, who sees that he has 'touched a tender point,' you may not go to the length of smashing furniture, but you have had a fire, and your dignity is damaged. You admit it to yourself afterwards. I am sure you know what I mean. And I am nearly sure that you, with your courageous candor, will admit that from time to time you suffer from these mysterious 'fires.'

'Temper,' one of the plagues of human society, is generally held to be incurable, save by the vague process of exercising self-control--a process which seldom has any beneficial results. It is regarded now as smallpox used to be regarded--as a visitation of Providence, which must be borne. But I do not hold it to be incurable. I am convinced that it is permanently curable. And its eminent importance as a nuisance to mankind at large deserves, I think, that it should receive particular attention. Anyhow, I am strongly against the visitation of Providence theory, as being unscientific, primitive, and conducive to unashamed laissez-aller. A man can be master in his own house. If he cannot be master by simple force of will, he can be master by ruse and wile. I would employ cleverness to maintain the throne of reason when it is likely to be upset in the mind by one of these devastating and disgraceful insurrections of brute instinct.

It is useless for a man in the habit of losing or mislaying his temper to argue with himself that such a proceeding is folly, that it serves no end, and does nothing but harm. It is useless for him to argue that in allowing his temper to stray he is probably guilty of cruelty, and certainly guilty of injustice to those persons who are forced to witness the loss. It is useless for him to argue that a man of uncertain temper in a house is like a man who goes about a house with a loaded revolver sticking from his pocket, and that all considerations of fairness and reason have to be subordinated in that house to the fear of the revolver, and that such peace as is maintained in that house is often a shameful and an unjust peace. These arguments will not be strong enough to prevail against one of the most powerful and capricious of all habits. This habit must be met and conquered (and it _can_ be!) by an even more powerful quality in the human mind; I mean the universal human horror of looking ridiculous. The man who loses his temper often thinks he is doing something rather fine and majestic. On the contrary, so far is this from being the fact, he is merely making an ass of himself. He is merely parading himself as an undignified fool, as that supremely contemptible figure--a grown-up baby. He may intimidate a feeble companion by his raging, or by the dark sullenness of a more subdued flame, but in the heart of even the weakest companion is a bedrock feeling of contempt for him. The way in which a man of uncertain temper is treated by his friends proves that they despise him, for they do not treat him as a reasonable being. How should they treat him as a reasonable being when the tenure of his reason is so insecure? And if only he could hear what is said of him behind his back!

The invalid can cure himself by teaching his brain the habit of dwelling upon his extreme fatuity. Let him concentrate regularly, with intense fixation, upon the ideas: 'When I lose my temper, when I get ruffled, when that mysterious vibration runs through me, I am making a donkey of myself, a donkey, and a donkey! You understand, a preposterous donkey! I am behaving like a great baby. I look a fool. I am a spectacle bereft of dignity. Everybody despises me, smiles at me in secret, disdains the idiotic ass with whom it is impossible to reason.'

Ordinarily the invalid disguises from himself this aspect of his disease, and his brain will instinctively avoid it as much as it can. But in hours of calm he can slowly and regularly force his brain, by the practice of concentration, to familiarize itself with just this aspect, so that in time its instinct will be to think first, and not last, of just this aspect. When he has arrived at that point he is saved. No man who, at the very inception of the fire, is visited with a clear vision of himself as an errant ass and pitiable object of contempt, will lack the volition to put the fire out. But, be it noted, he will not succeed until he can do it at once. A fire is a fire, and the engines must gallop by themselves out of the station instantly. This means the acquirement of a mental habit. During the preliminary stages of the cure he should, of course, avoid inflammable situations. This is a perfectly simple thing to do, if the brain has been disciplined out of its natural forgetfulness.

Chapter X

Mischievously Overworking It

I have dealt with the two general major causes of friction in the daily use of the machine. I will now deal with a minor cause, and make an end of mere dailiness. This minor cause--and after all I do not know that its results are so trifling as to justify the epithet 'minor'--is the straining of the machine by forcing it to do work which it was never intended to do. Although we are incapable of persuading our machines to do effectively that which they are bound to do somehow, we continually overburden them with entirely unnecessary and inept tasks. We cannot, it would seem, let things alone.

For example, in the ordinary household the amount of machine horse-power expended in fighting for the truth is really quite absurd. This pure zeal for the establishment and general admission of the truth is usually termed 'contradictoriness.' But, of course, it is not that; it is something higher. My wife states that the Joneses have gone into a new flat, of which the rent is L165 a year. Now, Jones has told me personally that the rent of his new flat is L156 a year. I correct my wife. Knowing that she is in the right, she corrects me. She cannot bear that a falsehood should prevail. It is not a question of L9, it is a question of truth. Her enthusiasm for truth excites my enthusiasm for truth. Five minutes ago I didn't care two pence whether the rent of the Joneses' new flat was L165 or L156 or L1056 a year. But now I care intensely that it is L156. I have formed myself into a select society for the propagating of the truth about the rent of the Joneses' new flat, and my wife has done the same. In eloquence,

85

in argumentative skill, in strict supervision of our tempers, we each of us squander enormous quantities of that h.-p. which is so precious to us. And the net effect is naught.

Now, if one of us two had understood the elementary principles of human engineering, that one would have said (privately): 'Truth is indestructible. Truth will out. Truth is never in a hurry. If it doesn't come out to-day it will come out to-morrow or next year. It can take care of itself. Ultimately my wife (or my husband) will learn the essential cosmic truth about the rent of the Joneses' new flat. I already know it, and the moment when she (or he) knows it also will be the moment of my triumph. She (or he) will not celebrate my triumph openly, but it will be none the less real. And my reputation for accuracy and calm restraint will be consolidated. If, by a rare mischance, I am in error, it will be vastly better for me in the day of my undoing that I have not been too positive now. Besides, nobody has appointed me sole custodian of the great truth concerning the rent of the Joneses' new flat. I was not brought into the world to be a safe-deposit, and more urgent matters summon me to effort.' If one of us had meditated thus, much needless friction would have been avoided and power saved; _amour-propre_ would not have been exposed to risks; the sacred cause of truth would not in the least have suffered; and the rent of the Joneses' new flat would anyhow have remained exactly what it is.

In addition to straining the machine by our excessive anxiety for the spread of truth, we give a very great deal too much attention to the state of other people's machines. I cannot too strongly, too sarcastically, deprecate this astonishing habit. It will be found to be rife in nearly every household and in nearly every office. We are most of us endeavoring to rearrange the mechanism in other heads than our own. This is always dangerous and generally futile. Considering the difficulty we have in our own brains, where our efforts are sure of being accepted as well-meant, and where we have at any rate a rough notion of the machine's construction, our intrepidity in adventuring among the delicate adjustments of other brains is remarkable. We are cursed by too much of the missionary spirit. We must needs voyage into the China of our brother's brain, and explain there that things are seriously wrong in that heathen land, and make ourselves unpleasant in the hope of getting them put right. We have all our own brain and body on which to wreak our personality, but this is not enough; we must extend our personality further, just as though we were a colonizing world-power intoxicated by the idea of the 'white man's burden.'

One of the central secrets of efficient daily living is to leave our daily companions alone a great deal more than we do, and attend to ourselves. If a daily companion is conducting his life upon principles which you know to be false, and with results which you feel to be unpleasant, the safe rule is to keep your mouth shut. Or if, out of your singular conceit, you are compelled to open it, open it with all precautions, and with the formal politeness you would use to a stranger. Intimacy is no excuse for rough manners, though the majority of us seem to think it is. You are not in charge of the universe; you are in charge of yourself. You cannot hope to manage the universe in your spare time, and if you try you will probably make a mess of such part of the universe as you touch, while gravely neglecting yourself. In every family there is generally someone whose meddlesome interest in other machines leads to serious friction in his own. Criticize less, even in the secrecy of your chamber. And do not blame at all. Accept your environment and adapt yourself to it in silence, instead of noisily attempting to adapt your environment to yourself. Here is true wisdom. You have no business trespassing beyond the confines of your own individuality. In so trespassing you are guilty of impertinence. This is obvious. And yet one of the chief activities of home-life consists in prancing about at random on other people's private lawns. What I say applies even to the relation between parents and children. And though my precept is exaggerated, it is purposely exaggerated in order effectively to balance the exaggeration in the opposite direction.

87

All individualities, other than one's own, are part of one's environment. The evolutionary process is going on all right, and they are a portion of it. Treat them as inevitable. To assert that they are inevitable is not to assert that they are unalterable. Only the alteration of them is not primarily your affair; it is theirs. Your affair is to use them, as they are, without self-righteousness, blame, or complaint, for the smooth furtherance of your own ends. There is no intention here to rob them of responsibility by depriving them of free-will while saddling _you_ with responsibility as a free agent. As your environment they must be accepted as inevitable, because they _are_ inevitable. But as centers themselves they have their own responsibility: which is not yours. The historic question: 'Have we free-will, or are we the puppets of determinism?' enters now. As a question it is fascinating and futile. It has never been, and it never will be, settled. The theory of determinism cannot be demolished by argument. But in his heart every man, including the most obstinate supporter of the theory, demolishes it every hour of every day. On the other hand, the theory of free-will can be demolished by ratiocination! So much the worse for ratiocination! _If we regard ourselves as free agents, and the personalities surrounding us as the puppets of determinism_, we shall have arrived at the working compromise from which the finest results of living can be obtained. The philosophic experience of centuries, if it has proved anything, has proved this. And the man who acts upon it in the common, banal contracts and collisions of the difficult experiment which we call daily life, will speedily become convinced of its practical worth.

Chapter XI

An Interlude

For ten chapters you have stood it, but not without protest. I know the feeling which is in your minds, and which has manifested itself in numerous criticisms of my ideas. That feeling may be briefly translated, perhaps, thus: 'This is all very well, but it isn't true, not a bit! It's only a fairy-tale that you have been telling us. Miracles don't happen,' etc. I, on my part, have a feeling that unless I take your feeling in hand at once, and firmly deal with it, I had better put my shutters up, for you will have got into the way of regarding me simply as a source of idle amusement. Already I can perceive, from the expressions of some critics, that, so far as they are concerned, I might just as well not have written a word. Therefore at this point I pause, in order to insist once more upon what I began by saying.

The burden of your criticism is: 'Human nature is always the same. I know my faults. But it is useless to tell me about them. I can't alter them. I was born like that.' The fatal weakness of this argument is, first, that it is based on a complete falsity; and second, that it puts you in an untenable position. Human nature _does_ change. Nothing can be more unscientific, more hopelessly mediaeval, than to imagine that it does not. It changes like everything else. You can't see it change. True! But then you can't see the grass growing--not unless you arise very early.

Is human nature the same now as in the days of Babylonian civilization, when the social machine was oiled by drenchings of blood? Is it the same now as in the days of Greek civilization, when there was no such thing as romantic love between the sexes? Is it the same now as it was during the centuries when constant friction had to provide its own cure in the shape of constant war? Is it the same now as it was on 2nd March 1819, when the British Government officially opposed a motion to consider the severity of the criminal laws (which included capital punishment for cutting down a tree, and other sensible dodges against friction), and were defeated by a majority of only nineteen votes? Is it the same now as in the year 1883, when the first S.P.C.C. was formed in England?

If you consider that human nature is still the same you should instantly go out and make a bonfire of the works of Spencer, Darwin, and Wallace, and then return to enjoy the purely jocular side of the present volume. If you admit that it has changed, let me ask you how it has changed, unless by the continual infinitesimal efforts, _upon themselves_, of individual men, like you and me. Did you suppose it was changed by magic, or by Acts of Parliament, or by the action of groups on persons, and not of persons on groups? Let me tell you that human nature has changed since yesterday. Let me tell you that to-day reason has a more powerful voice in the directing of instinct than it had yesterday. Let me tell you that to-day the friction of the machines is less screechy and grinding than it was yesterday.

'You were born like that, and you can't alter yourself, and so it's no use talking.' If you really believe this, why make any effort at all? Why not let the whole business beautifully slide and yield to your instincts? What object can there be in trying to control yourself in any manner whatever if you are unalterable? Assert yourself to be unalterable, and you assert yourself a fatalist. Assert yourself a fatalist, and you free yourself from all moral responsibility--and other people, too. Well, then, act up to your convictions, if convictions they are. If you can't alter yourself, I can't alter myself, and supposing that I come along and bash you on the head and steal your purse, you can't blame me. You can only, on recovering consciousness, affectionately grasp my hand

90

and murmur: 'Don't apologize, my dear fellow; we can't alter ourselves.'

This, you say, is absurd. It is. That is one of my innumerable points. The truth is, you do not really believe that you cannot alter yourself. What is the matter with you is just what is the matter with me--sheer idleness. You hate getting up in the morning, and to excuse your inexcusable indolence you talk big about Fate. Just as 'patriotism is the last refuge of a scoundrel,' so fatalism is the last refuge of a shirker. But you deceive no one, least of all yourself. You have not, rationally, a leg to stand on. At this juncture, because I have made you laugh, you consent to say: 'I do try, all I can. But I can only alter myself a very little. By constitution I am mentally idle. I can't help that, can I?' Well, so long as you are not the only absolutely unchangeable thing in a universe of change, I don't mind. It is something for you to admit that you can alter yourself even a very little. The difference between our philosophies is now only a question of degree.

In the application of any system of perfecting the machine, no two persons will succeed equally. From the disappointed tone of some of your criticisms it might be fancied that I had advertised a system for making archangels out of tailors' dummies. Such was not my hope. I have no belief in miracles. But I know that when a thing is thoroughly well done it often has the air of being a miracle. My sole aim is to insist that every man shall perfect his machine to the best of _his_ powers, not to the best of somebody else's powers. I do not indulge in any hope that a man can be better than his best self. I am, however, convinced that every man fails to be his best self a great deal oftener than he need fail--for the reason that his will-power, be it great or small, is not directed according to the principles of common sense.

Common sense will surely lead a man to ask the question: 'Why did my actions yesterday contradict my reason?' The reply to this question will nearly always be: 'Because at the critical moment I forgot.' The supreme explanation of the abortive results of so many efforts at self-alteration, the supreme explanation of our frequent miserable scurrying into a doctrine of fatalism, is simple forgetfulness. It is not force that we lack, but the skill to remember exactly what our reason would have us do or think at the moment itself. How is this skill to be acquired? It can only be acquired, as skill at games is acquired, by practice; by the training of the organ involved to such a point that the organ acts rightly by instinct instead of wrongly by instinct. There are degrees of success in this procedure, but there is no such phenomenon as complete failure.

Habits which increase friction can be replaced by habits which lessen friction. Habits which arrest development can be replaced by habits which encourage development. And as a habit is formed naturally, so it can be formed artificially, by imitation of the unconscious process, by accustoming the brain to the new idea. Let me, as an example, refer again to the minor subject of daily friction, and, within that subject, to the influence of tone. A man employs a frictional tone through habit. The frictional tone is an instinct with him. But if he had a quarter of an hour to reflect before speaking, and if during that quarter of an hour he could always listen to arguments against the frictional tone, his use of the frictional tone would rapidly diminish; his reason would conquer his instinct. As things are, his instinct conquers his reason by a surprise attack, by taking it unawares. Regular daily concentration of the brain, for a certain period, upon the non-frictional tone, and the immense advantages of its use, will gradually set up in the brain a new habit of thinking about the non-frictional tone; until at length the brain, disciplined, turns to the correct act before the old, silly instinct can capture it; and ultimately a new sagacious instinct will supplant the old one.

This is the rationale. It applies to all habits. Any person can test its efficiency in any habit. I care not whether he be of strong or weak will--he can test it. He will soon see the tremendous difference between merely 'making a good resolution'--(he has been doing that all his life without any very brilliant consequences)--and concentrating the brain for a given time exclusively upon a good resolution. Concentration, the efficient mastery of the brain--all is there!

Chapter XII

An Interest in Life

After a certain period of mental discipline, of deliberate habit-forming and habit-breaking, such as I have been indicating, a man will begin to acquire at any rate a superficial knowledge, a nodding acquaintance, with that wonderful and mysterious affair, his brain, and he will also begin to perceive how important a factor in daily life is the control of his brain. He will assuredly be surprised at the miracles which lie between his collar and his hat, in that queer box that he calls his head. For the effects that can be accomplished by mere steady, persistent thinking must appear to be miracles to apprentices in the practice of thought. When once a man, having passed an unhappy day because his clumsy, negligent brain forgot to control his instincts at a critical moment, has said to his brain: 'I will force you, by concentrating you on that particular point, to act efficiently the next time similar circumstances arise,' and when he has carried out his intention, and when the awkward circumstances have recurred, and his brain, disciplined, has done its work, and so prevented unhappiness--then that man will regard his brain with a new eye. 'By Jove!' he will say; 'I've stopped one source of unhappiness, anyway. There was a time when I should have made a fool of myself in a little domestic crisis such as today's. But I have gone safely through it. I am all right. She is all right. The atmosphere is not dangerous with undischarged electricity! And all because my brain, being in proper condition, watched firmly over my instincts! I must keep this up.' He will peer into that brain more and more. He will see

94

more and more of its possibilities. He will have a new and a supreme interest in _life_. A garden is a fairly interesting thing. But the cultivation of a garden is as dull as cold mutton compared to the cultivation of a brain; and wet weather won't interfere with digging, planting, and pruning in the box.

In due season the man whose hobby is his brain will gradually settle down into a daily routine, with which routine he will start the day. The idea at the back of the mind of the ordinary man (by the ordinary man I mean the man whose brain is not his hobby) is almost always this: 'There are several things at present hanging over me--worries, unfulfilled ambitions, unrealized desires. As soon as these things are definitely settled, then I shall begin to live and enjoy myself.' That is the ordinary man's usual idea. He has it from his youth to his old age. He is invariably waiting for something to happen before he really begins to live. I am sure that if you are an ordinary man (of course, you aren't, I know) you will admit that this is true of you; you exist in the hope that one day things will be sufficiently smoothed out for you to begin to live. That is just where you differ from the man whose brain is his hobby. His daily routine consists in a meditation in the following vein: 'This day is before me. The circumstances of this day are my environment; they are the material out of which, by means of my brain, I have to live and be happy and to refrain from causing unhappiness in other people. It is the business of my brain to make use of _this_ material. My brain is in its box for that sole purpose. Not to-morrow! Not next year! Not when I have made my fortune! Not when my sick child is out of danger! Not when my wife has returned to her senses! Not when my salary is raised! Not when I have passed that examination! Not when my indigestion is better! But _now!_ To-day, exactly as to-day is! The facts of to-day, which in my unregeneracy I regarded primarily as anxieties, nuisances, impediments, I now regard as so much raw material from which my brain has to weave a tissue of life that is comely.'

95

And then he foresees the day as well as he can. His experience teaches him where he will have difficulty, and he administers to his brain the lessons of which it will have most need. He carefully looks the machine over, and arranges it especially for the sort of road which he knows that it will have to traverse. And especially he readjusts his point of view, for his point of view is continually getting wrong. He is continually seeing worries where he ought to see material. He may notice, for instance, a patch on the back of his head, and he wonders whether it is the result of age or of disease, or whether it has always been there. And his wife tells him he must call at the chemist's and satisfy himself at once. Frightful nuisance! Age! The endless trouble of a capillary complaint! Calling at the chemist's will make him late at the office! etc. etc. But then his skilled, efficient brain intervenes: 'What peculiarly interesting material this mean and petty circumstance yields for the practice of philosophy and right living!' And again: 'Is _this_ to ruffle you, O my soul? Will it serve any end whatever that I should buzz nervously round this circumstance instead of attending to my usual business?'

I give this as an example of the necessity of adjusting the point of view, and of the manner in which a brain habituated by suitable concentration to correct thinking will come to the rescue in unexpected contingencies. Naturally it will work with greater certainty in the manipulation of difficulties that are expected, that can be 'seen coming '; and preparation for the expected is, fortunately, preparation for the unexpected. The man who commences his day by a steady contemplation of the dangers which the next sixteen hours are likely to furnish, and by arming himself especially against those dangers, has thereby armed himself, though to a less extent, against dangers which he did not dream of. But the routine must be fairly elastic. It may be necessary to commence several days in succession--for a week or for months, even--with disciplining the brain in one particular detail, to the temporary neglect of other matters. It is astonishing how you can weed every inch of a garden path and keep it in the most meticulous order, and then one morning find

96

in the very middle of it a lusty, full-grown plant whose roots are positively mortised in granite! All gardeners are familiar with such discoveries.

But a similar discovery, though it entails hard labor on him, will not disgust the man whose hobby is his brain. For the discovery in itself is part of the material out of which he has to live. If a man is to turn everything whatsoever into his own calm, dignity, and happiness, he must make this use even of his own failures. He must look at them as phenomena of the brain in that box, and cheerfully set about taking measures to prevent their repetition. All that happens to him, success or check, will but serve to increase his interest in the contents of that box. I seem to hear you saying: 'And a fine egotist he'll be!' Well, he'll be the right sort of egotist. The average man is not half enough of an egotist. If egotism means a terrific interest in one's self, egotism is absolutely essential to efficient living. There is no getting away from that. But if egotism means selfishness, the serious student of the craft of daily living will not be an egotist for more than about a year. In a year he will have proved the ineptitude of egotism.

Chapter XIII

Success and Failure

I am sadly aware that these brief chapters will be apt to convey, especially to the trustful and enthusiastic reader, a false impression; the impression of simplicity; and that when experience has roughly corrected this impression, the said reader, unless he is most solemnly warned, may abandon the entire enterprise in a fit of disgust, and forever afterwards maintain a cynical and impolite attitude towards all theories of controlling the human machine. Now, the enterprise is not a simple one. It is based on one simple principle--the conscious discipline of the brain by selected habits of thought--but it is just about as complicated as anything well could be. Advanced golf is child's play compared to it. The man who briefly says to himself: 'I will get up at 8, and from 8.30 to 9 I will examine and control my brain, and so my life will at once be instantly improved out of recognition'--that man is destined to unpleasant surprises. Progress will be slow. Progress may appear to be quite rapid at first, and then a period of futility may set in, and the would-be vanquisher of his brain may suffer a series of the most deadly defeats. And in his pessimism he may imagine that all his pains have gone for nothing, and that the unserious loungers in exhibition gardens and readers of novels in parlors are in the right of it after all. He may even feel rather ashamed of himself for having been, as he thinks, taken in by specious promises, like the purchaser of a quack medicine.

The conviction that great effort has been made and no progress achieved is the chief of the dangers that affront the beginner in machine-tending. It is, I will assert positively, in every case a

98

conviction unjustified by the facts, and usually it is the mere result of reaction after fatigue, encouraged by the instinct for laziness. I do not think it will survive an impartial examination; but I know that a man, in order to find an excuse for abandoning further effort, is capable of convincing himself that past effort has yielded no fruit at all. So curious is the human machine. I beg every student of himself to consider this remark with all the intellectual honesty at his disposal. It is a grave warning.

When the machine-tender observes that he is frequently changing his point of view; when he notices that what he regarded as the kernel of the difficulty yesterday has sunk to a triviality to-day, being replaced by a fresh phenomenon; when he arises one morning and by means of a new, unexpected glimpse into the recesses of the machine perceives that hitherto he has been quite wrong and must begin again; when he wonders how on earth he could have been so blind and so stupid as not to see what now he sees; when the new vision is veiled by new disappointments and narrowed by continual reservations; when he is overwhelmed by the complexity of his undertaking-- then let him unhearten himself, for he is succeeding. The history of success in any art--and machine-tending is an art--is a history of recommencements, of the dispersal and reforming of doubts, of an ever-increasing conception of the extent of the territory unconquered, and an ever-decreasing conception of the extent of the territory conquered.

It is remarkable that, though no enterprise could possibly present more diverse and changeful excitements than the mastering of the brain, the second great danger which threatens its ultimate success is nothing but a mere drying-up of enthusiasm for it! One would have thought that in an affair which concerned him so nearly, in an affair whose results might be in a very strict sense vital to him, in an affair upon which his happiness and misery might certainly turn, a man would not weary from sheer tedium. Nevertheless, it is so. Again and again I have noticed the abandonment, temporary or permanent, of this mighty and thrilling enterprise from simple lack of interest. And I imagine that, in practically all cases save those in which an exceptional original force of will renders the enterprise scarcely necessary, the interest in it will languish unless it is regularly nourished from without. Now, the interest in it cannot be nourished from without by means of conversation with other brain-tamers. There are certain things which may not be discussed by sanely organized people; and this is one. The affair is too intimate, and it is also too moral. Even after only a few minutes' vocalization on this subject a deadly infection seems to creep into the air--the infection of priggishness. (Or am I mistaken, and do I fancy this horror? No; I cannot believe that I am mistaken.)

Hence the nourishment must be obtained by reading; a little reading every day. I suppose there are some thousands of authors who have written with more or less sincerity on the management of the human machine. But the two which, for me, stand out easily above all the rest are Marcus Aurelius Antoninus and Epictetus. Not much has been discovered since their time. 'The perfecting of life is a power residing in the soul,' wrote Marcus Aurelius in the ninth book of "To Himself", over seventeen hundred years ago. Marcus Aurelius is assuredly regarded as the greatest of writers in the human machine school, and not to read him daily is considered by many to be a bad habit. As a confession his work stands alone. But as a practical 'Bradshaw' of existence, I would put the discourses of Epictetus before M. Aurelius. Epictetus is grosser; he will call you a blockhead as soon as look at you; he is witty, he is even humorous, and he never wanders far away from the incidents of daily life. He is brimming over with actuality for readers of the year 1908. He was a freed slave. M. Aurelius was an emperor, and he had the morbidity from which all emperors must suffer. A finer soul than Epictetus, he is not, in my view, so useful a companion. Not all of us can breathe freely in his atmosphere. Nevertheless, he is of course to be read, and re-read continually. When you have gone through Epictetus--a single page or paragraph per day, well masticated and digested, suffices--you can go through M. Aurelius, and then you can return to Epictetus, and so on, morning by morning, or night by night, till your life's end. And they will conserve your interest in yourself.

In the matter of concentration, I hesitate to recommend Mrs. Annie Besant's _Thought Power_, and yet I should be possibly unjust if I did not recommend it, having regard to its immense influence on myself. It is not one of the best books of this astounding woman. It is addressed to theosophists, and can only be completely understood in the light of Theosophistic doctrines. (To grasp it all I found myself obliged to study a much larger work dealing with theosophy as a whole.) It contains an appreciable quantity of what strikes me as feeble sentimentalism, and also a lot of sheer dogma. But it is the least unsatisfactory manual of the brain that I have met with. And if the profane reader ignores all that is either Greek or twaddle to him, there will yet remain for his advantage a vast amount of very sound information and advice. All these three books are cheap.

Chapter XIV

A Man and His Environment

I now come to an entirely different aspect of the whole subject. Hitherto I have dealt with the human machine as a contrivance for adapting the man to his environment. My aim has been to show how much depends on the machine and how little depends on the environment, and that the essential business of the machine is to utilize, for making the stuff of life, the particular environment in which it happens to find itself--and no other! All this, however, does not imply that one must accept, fatalistically and permanently and passively, any preposterous environment into which destiny has chanced to throw us. If we carry far enough the discipline of our brains, we can, no doubt, arrive at surprisingly good results in no matter what environment. But it would not be 'right reason' to expend an excessive amount of will-power on brain-discipline when a slighter effort in a different direction would produce consequences more felicitous. A man whom fate had pitched into a canal might accomplish miracles in the way of rendering himself amphibian; he might stagger the world by the spectacle of his philosophy under amazing difficulties; people might pay sixpence a head to come and see him; but he would be less of a nincompoop if he climbed out and arranged to live definitely on the bank.

The advantage of an adequate study of the control of the machine, such as I have outlined, is that it enables the student to judge, with some certainty, whether the unsatisfactoriness of his life is caused by a disordered machine or by an environment for which the machine is, in its fundamental construction, unsuitable. It does help him to decide justly whether, in the case of a grave difference between them, he, or the rest of the universe, is in the wrong. And also, if he decides that he is not in the wrong, it helps him to choose a new environment, or to modify the old, upon some scientific principle. The vast majority of people never know, with any precision, why they are dissatisfied with their sojourn on this planet. They make long and fatiguing excursions in search of precious materials which all the while are concealed in their own breasts. They don't know what they want; they only know that they want something. Or, if they contrive to settle in their own minds what they do want, a hundred to one the obtaining of it will leave them just as far off contentment as they were at the beginning! This is a matter of daily observation: that people are frantically engaged in attempting to get hold of things which, by universal experience, are hideously disappointing to those who have obtained possession of them. And still the struggle goes on, and probably will go on. All because brains are lying idle! 'It is no trifle that is at stake,' said Epictetus as to the question of control of instinct by reason. '_It means, Are you in your senses or are you not_?' In this significance, indubitably the vast majority of people are not in their senses; otherwise they would not behave as they do, so vaguely, so happy-go-luckily, so blindly. But the man whose brain is in working order emphatically _is_ in his senses.

And when a man, by means of the efficiency of his brain, has put his reason in definite command over his instincts, he at once sees things in a truer perspective than was before possible, and therefore he is able to set a just value upon the various parts which go to make up his environment. If, for instance, he lives in London, and is aware of constant friction, he will be led to examine the claims of London as a Mecca for intelligent persons. He may say to himself: 'There is something wrong, and the seat of trouble is not in the machine. London compels me to tolerate dirt, darkness, ugliness, strain, tedious daily journeyings, and general expensiveness. What does London give me in exchange?' And he may decide that, as London offers him nothing special in exchange except the glamour of London and an occasional seat at a good concert or a bad play, he may get a better return for his expenditure of brains, nerves, and money in the provinces. He may perceive, with a certain French novelist, that 'most people of truly distinguished mind prefer the provinces.' And he may then actually, in obedience to reason, quit the deceptions of London with a tranquil heart, sure of his diagnosis. Whereas a man who had not devoted much time to the care of his mental machinery could not screw himself up to the step, partly from lack of resolution, and partly because he had never examined the sources of his unhappiness. A man who, not having full control of his machine, is consistently dissatisfied with his existence, is like a man who is being secretly poisoned and cannot decide with what or by whom. And so he has no middle course between absolute starvation and a continuance of poisoning.

As with the environment of place, so with the environment of individuals. Most friction between individuals is avoidable friction; sometimes, however, friction springs from such deep causes that no skill in the machine can do away with it. But how is the man whose brain is not in command of his existence to judge whether the unpleasantness can be cured or not, whether it arises in himself or in the other? He simply cannot judge. Whereas a man who keeps his brain for use and not for idle amusement will, when he sees that friction persists in spite of his brain, be so clearly impressed by the advisability of separation as the sole cure that he will steel himself to the effort necessary for a separation. One of the chief advantages of an efficient brain is that an efficient brain is capable of acting with firmness and resolution, partly, of course, because it has been toned up, but more because its operations are not confused by the interference of mere instincts.

Thirdly, there is the environment of one's general purpose in life, which is, I feel convinced, far more often hopelessly wrong and futile than either the environment of situation or the environment of individuals. I will be bold enough to say that quite seventy per cent of ambition is never realized at all, and that ninety-nine per cent of all realized ambition is fruitless. In other words, that a gigantic sacrifice of the present to the future is always going on. And here again the utility of brain-discipline is most strikingly shown. A man whose first business it is every day to concentrate his mind on the proper performance of that particular day, must necessarily conserve his interest in the present. It is impossible that his perspective should become so warped that he will devote, say, fifty-five years of his career to problematical preparations for his comfort and his glory during the final ten years. A man whose brain is his servant, and not his lady-help or his pet dog, will be in receipt of such daily content and satisfaction that he will early ask himself the question: 'As for this ambition that is eating away my hours, what will it give me that I have not already got?' Further, the steady development of interest in the hobby (call it!) of common-sense daily living will act as an automatic test of any ambition. If an ambition survives and flourishes on the top of that daily cultivation of the machine, then the owner of the ambition may be sure that it is a genuine and an invincible ambition, and he may pursue it in full faith; his developed care for the present will prevent him from making his ambition an altar on which the whole of the present is to be offered up.

I shall be told that I want to do away with ambition, and that ambition is the great motive-power of existence, and that therefore I am an enemy of society and the truth is not in me. But I do not want to do away with ambition. What I say is that current ambitions usually result in disappointment, that they usually mean the complete distortion of a life. This is an incontestable fact, and the reason of it is that ambitions are chosen either without knowledge of their real value or without knowledge of what they will cost. A disciplined brain will at once show the unnecessariness of most ambitions, and will ensure that the remainder shall be conducted with reason. It will also convince its possessor that the ambition to live strictly according to the highest common sense during the next twenty-four hours is an ambition that needs a lot of beating.

Chapter XV

L.S.D.

Anybody who really wishes to talk simple truth about money at the present time is confronted by a very serious practical difficulty. He must put himself in opposition to the overwhelming body of public opinion, and resign himself to being regarded either as a poseur, a crank, or a fool. The public is in search of happiness now, as it was a million years ago. Money is not the principal factor in happiness. It may be argued whether, as a factor in happiness, money is of twentieth-rate importance or fiftieth-rate importance. But it cannot be argued whether money, in point of fact, does or does not of itself bring happiness. There can be no doubt whatever that money does not bring happiness. Yet, in face of this incontrovertible and universal truth, the whole public behaves exactly as if money were the sole or the principal preliminary to happiness. The public does not reason, and it will not listen to reason; its blood is up in the money-hunt, and the philosopher might as well expostulate with an earthquake as try to take that public by the button-hole and explain. If a man sacrifices his interest under the will of some dead social tyrant in order to marry whom he wishes, if an English minister of religion declines twenty-five thousand dollars a year to go into exile and preach to New York millionaires, the phenomenon is genuinely held to be so astounding that it at once flies right round the world in the form of exclamatory newspaper articles! In an age when such an attitude towards money is sincere, it is positively dangerous--I doubt if it may not be harmful--to persist with loud obstinacy that money, instead of being the greatest, is the least thing in the world. In times of high military excitement a man may be ostracized if not lynched for uttering opinions which everybody will accept as truisms a couple of years later, and thus the wise philosopher holds his tongue--lest it should be cut out. So at the zenith of a period when the possession of money in absurd masses is an infallible means to the general respect, I have no intention either of preaching or of practicing quite all that I privately in the matter of riches.

It was not always thus. Though there have been previous ages as lustful for wealth and ostentation as our own, there have also been ages when money-getting and millionaire-envying were not the sole preoccupations of the average man. And such an age will undoubtedly succeed to ours. Few things would surprise me less, in social life, than the upspringing of some anti-luxury movement, the formation of some league or guild among the middling classes (where alone intellect is to be found in quantity), the members of which would bind themselves to stand aloof from all the great, silly, banal, ugly, and tedious _luxe_-activities of the time and not to spend more than a certain sum per annum on eating, drinking, covering their bodies, and being moved about like parcels from one spot of the earth's surface to another. Such a movement would, and will, help towards the formation of an opinion which would condemn lavish expenditure on personal satisfactions as bad form. However, the shareholders of grand hotels, restaurants, and race-courses of all sorts, together with popular singers and barristers, etc., need feel no immediate alarm. The movement is not yet.

As touching the effect of money on the efficient ordering of the human machine, there is happily no necessity to inform those who have begun to interest themselves in the conduct of their own brains that money counts for very little in that paramount affair. Nothing that really helps towards perfection costs more than is within the means of every person who reads these pages. The expenses connected with daily meditation, with the

108

building-up of mental habits, with the practice of self-control and of cheerfulness, with the enthronement of reason over the rabble of primeval instincts--these expenses are really, you know, trifling. And whether you get that well-deserved rise of a pound a week or whether you don't, you may anyhow go ahead with the machine; it isn't a motor-car, though I started by comparing it to one. And even when, having to a certain extent mastered, through sensible management of the machine, the art of achieving a daily content and dignity, you come to the embroidery of life--even the best embroidery of life is not absolutely ruinous. Meat may go up in price--it has done--but books won't. Admission to picture galleries and concerts and so forth will remain quite low. The views from Richmond Hill or Hindhead, or along Pall Mall at sunset, the smell of the earth, the taste of fruit and of kisses--these things are unaffected by the machinations of trusts and the hysteria of stock exchanges. Travel, which after books is the finest of all embroideries (and which is not to be valued by the mile but by the quality), is decidedly cheaper than ever it was. All that is required is ingenuity in one's expenditure. And much ingenuity with a little money is vastly more profitable and amusing than much money without ingenuity.

And all the while as you read this you are saying, with your impatient sneer: 'It's all very well; it's all very fine talking, _but_ ...' In brief, you are not convinced. You cannot deracinate that wide-rooted dogma within your soul that more money means more joy. I regret it. But let me put one question, and let me ask you to answer it honestly. Your financial means are greater now than they used to be. Are you happier or less discontented than you used to be? Taking your existence day by day, hour by hour, judging it by the mysterious _feel_ (in the chest) of responsibilities, worries, positive joys and satisfactions, are you genuinely happier than you used to be?

I do not wish to be misunderstood. The financial question cannot be ignored. If it is true that money does not bring happiness, it is no less true that the lack of money induces a state of affairs in which efficient living becomes doubly difficult. These two propositions, superficially perhaps self-contradictory, are not really so. A modest income suffices for the fullest realization of the Ego in terms of content and dignity; but you must live within it. You cannot righteously ignore money. A man, for instance, who cultivates himself and instructs a family of daughters in everything except the ability to earn their own livelihood, and then has the impudence to die suddenly without leaving a penny--that man is a scoundrel. Ninety--or should I say ninety-nine?--per cent. of all those anxieties which render proper living almost impossible are caused by the habit of walking on the edge of one's income as one might walk on the edge of a precipice. The majority of Englishmen have some financial worry or other continually, everlastingly at the back of their minds. The sacrifice necessary to abolish this condition of things is more apparent than real. All spending is a matter of habit.

Speaking generally, a man can contrive, out of an extremely modest income, to have all that he needs--unless he needs the esteem of snobs. Habit may, and habit usually does, make it just as difficult to keep a family on two thousand a year as on two hundred. I suppose that for the majority of men the suspension of income for a single month would mean either bankruptcy, the usurer, or acute inconvenience. Impossible, under such circumstances, to be in full and independent possession of one's immortal soul! Hence I should be inclined to say that the first preliminary to a proper control of the machine is the habit of spending decidedly less than one earns or receives. The veriest automaton of a clerk ought to have the wherewithal of a whole year as a shield against the caprices of his employer. It would be as reasonable to expect the inhabitants of an unfortified city in the midst of a plain occupied by a hostile army to apply themselves successfully to the study of logarithms or metaphysics, as to expect a man without a year's income in his safe to apply himself successfully to the true art of living.

And the whole secret of relative freedom from financial anxiety lies not in income, but in expenditure. I am ashamed to utter this antique platitude. But, like most aphorisms of unassailable wisdom, it is completely ignored. You say, of course, that it is not easy to leave a margin between your expenditure and your present income. I know it. I fraternally shake your hand. Still it is, in most cases, far easier to lessen one's expenditure than to increase one's income without increasing one's expenditure. The alternative is before you. However you decide, be assured that the foundation of philosophy is a margin, and that the margin can always be had.

Chapter XVI

Reason, Reason!

In conclusion, I must insist upon several results of what I may call the 'intensive culture' of the reason. The brain will not only grow more effectively powerful in the departments of life where the brain is supposed specially to work, but it will also enlarge the circle of its activities. It will assuredly interfere in everything. The student of himself must necessarily conduct his existence more and more according to the views of his brain. This will be most salutary and agreeable both for himself and for the rest of the world. You object. You say it will be a pity when mankind refers everything to reason. You talk about the heart. You envisage an entirely reasonable existence as a harsh and callous existence. Not so. When the reason and the heart come into conflict the heart is invariably wrong. I do not say that the reason is always entirely right, but I do say that it is always less wrong than the heart. The empire of the reason is not universal, but within its empire reason is supreme, and if other forces challenge it on its own soil they must take the consequences. Nearly always, when the heart opposes the brain, the heart is merely a pretty name which we give to our idleness and our egotism.

We pass along the Strand and see a respectable young widow standing in the gutter, with a baby in her arms and a couple of boxes of matches in one hand. We know she is a widow because of her weeds, and we know she is respectable by her clothes. We know she is not begging because she is selling matches. The sight of her in the gutter pains our heart. Our heart weeps and gives the woman a penny in exchange for a halfpenny box of matches, and the pain of our heart is thereby assuaged. Our heart has performed a good action. But later on our reason (unfortunately asleep at the moment) wakes up and says: 'That baby was hired; the weeds and matches merely a dodge. The whole affair was a spectacle got up to extract money from a fool like you. It is as mechanical as a penny in the slot. Instead of relieving distress you have simply helped to perpetuate an infamous system. You ought to know that you can't do good in that offhand way.' The heart gives pennies in the street. The brain runs the Charity Organization Society. Of course, to give pennies in the street is much less trouble than to run the C.O.S. As a method of producing a quick, inexpensive, and pleasing effect on one's egotism the C.O.S. is simply not in it with this dodge of giving pennies at random, without inquiry. Only-- which of the two devices ought to be accused of harshness and callousness? Which of them is truly kind? I bring forward the respectable young widow as a sample case of the Heart _v_. Brain conflict. All other cases are the same. The brain is always more kind than the heart; the brain is always more willing than the heart to put itself to a great deal of trouble for a very little reward; the brain always does the difficult, unselfish thing, and the heart always does the facile, showy thing. Naturally the result of the brain's activity on society is always more advantageous than the result of the heart's activity.

Another point. I have tried to show that, if the reason is put in command of the feelings, it is impossible to assume an attitude of blame towards any person whatsoever for any act whatsoever. The habit of blaming must depart absolutely. It is no argument against this statement that it involves anarchy and the demolition of society. Even if it did (which emphatically it does not), that would not affect its truth. All great truths have been assailed on the ground that to accept them meant the end of everything. As if that mattered! As I make no claim to be the discoverer of this truth I have no hesitation in announcing it to be one of the most important truths that the world has yet to learn. However, the real reason why many people object to this truth is not because they think it involves the utter demolition of society (fear of the utter demolition of society never stopped any one from doing or believing anything, and never will), but because they say to themselves that if they can't blame they can't praise. And they do so like praising! If they are so desperately fond of praising, it is a pity that they don't praise a little more! There can be no doubt that the average man blames much more than he praises. His instinct is to blame. If he is satisfied he says nothing; if he is not, he most illogically kicks up a row. So that even if the suppression of blame involved the suppression of praise the change would certainly be a change for the better. But I can perceive no reason why the suppression of blame should involve the suppression of praise. On the contrary, I think that the habit of praising should be fostered. (I do not suggest the occasional use of trowels, but the regular use of salt-spoons.) Anyhow, the triumph of the brain over the natural instincts (in an ideally organized man the brain and the natural instincts will never have even a tiff) always means the ultimate triumph of kindness.

And, further, the culture of the brain, the constant disciplinary exercise of the reasoning faculty, means the diminution of misdeeds. (Do not imagine I am hinting that you are on the verge of murdering your wife or breaking into your neighbor's house. Although you personally are guiltless, there is a good deal of sin still committed in your immediate vicinity.) Said Balzac in _La Cousine Bette_, 'A crime is in the first instance a defect of reasoning powers.' In the appreciation of this truth, Marcus Aurelius was, as usual, a bit beforehand with Balzac. M. Aurelius said, 'No soul willfully misses truth.' And Epictetus had come to the same conclusion before M. Aurelius, and Plato before Epictetus. All wrong-doing is done in the sincere belief that it is the best thing to do. Whatever sin a man does he does either for his own benefit or for the benefit of society. At the moment of doing it he is convinced that it is the only thing to do. He is mistaken. And he is mistaken because his brain has been unequal to the task of reasoning the matter out. Passion (the heart) is responsible for all crimes. Indeed, crime is simply a convenient monosyllable which we apply to what happens when the brain and the heart come into conflict and the brain is defeated. That transaction of the matches was a crime, you know.

Lastly, the culture of the brain must result in the habit of originally examining all the phenomena of life and conduct, to see what they really are, and to what they lead. The heart hates progress, because the dear old thing always wants to do as has always been done. The heart is convinced that custom is a virtue. The heart of the dirty working man rebels when the State insists that he shall be clean, for no other reason than that it is his custom to be dirty. Useless to tell his heart that, clean, he will live longer! He has been dirty and he will be. The brain alone is the enemy of prejudice and precedent, which alone are the enemies of progress. And this habit of originally examining phenomena is perhaps the greatest factor that goes to the making of personal dignity; for it fosters reliance on one's self and courage to accept the consequences of the act of reasoning. Reason is the basis of personal dignity.

I finish. I have said nothing of the modifications which the constant use of the brain will bring about in the _general value of existence_. Modifications slow and subtle, but tremendous! The persevering will discover them. It will happen to the persevering that their whole lives are changed--texture and color, too! Naught will happen to those who do not persevere.

Mental Efficiency

Chapter I
Mental Efficiency

THE APPEAL

If there is any virtue in advertisements--and a journalist should be the last person to say that there is not--the American nation is rapidly reaching a state of physical efficiency of which the world has probably not seen the like since Sparta. In all the American newspapers and all the American monthlies are innumerable illustrated announcements of "physical-culture specialists," who guarantee to make all the organs of the body perform their duties with the mighty precision of a 60 horse power motor-car that never breaks down. I saw a book the other day written by one of these specialists, to show how perfect health could be attained by devoting a quarter of an hour a day to certain exercises. The advertisements multiply and increase in size. They cost a great deal of money. Therefore they must bring in a great deal of business. Therefore vast numbers of people must be worried about the non-efficiency of their bodies, and on the way to achieve efficiency. In our more modest British fashion, we have the same phenomenon in England. And it is growing. Our muscles are growing also. Surprise a man in his bedroom of a morning, and you will find him lying on his back on the floor, or standing on his head, or whirling clubs, in pursuit of physical efficiency. I remember that once I "went in" for physical efficiency myself. I, too, lay on the floor, my delicate epidermis separated from the carpet by only the thinnest of garments, and I contorted myself according to the fifteen diagrams of a large chart (believed to be the "Magna Carta" of physical efficiency) daily after shaving. In three weeks my collars would not meet round my prize-fighter's neck; my hosier reaped immense profits, and I came to the conclusion that I had carried physical efficiency quite far enough.

A strange thing--was it not?--that I never had the idea of devoting a quarter of an hour a day after shaving to the pursuit of mental efficiency. The average body is a pretty complicated affair, sadly out of order, but happily susceptible to culture. The average mind is vastly more complicated, not less sadly out of order, but perhaps even more susceptible to culture. We compare our arms to the arms of the gentleman illustrated in the physical efficiency advertisement, and we murmur to ourselves the classic phrase: "This will never do." And we set about developing the muscles of our arms until we can show them off (through a frock coat) to women at afternoon tea. But it does not, perhaps, occur to us that the mind has its muscles, and a lot of apparatus besides, and that these invisible, yet paramount, mental organs are far less efficient than they ought to be; that some of them are atrophied, others starved, others out of shape, etc. A man of sedentary occupation goes for a very long walk on Easter Monday, and in the evening is so exhausted that he can scarcely eat. He wakes up to the inefficiency of his body, caused by his neglect of it, and he is so shocked that he determines on remedial measures. Either he will walk to the office, or he will play golf, or he will execute the post-shaving exercises. But let the same man after a prolonged sedentary course of newspapers, magazines, and novels, take his mind out for a stiff climb among the rocks of a scientific, philosophic, or artistic subject. What will he do? Will he stay out all day, and return in the evening too tired even to read his paper? Not he. It is ten to one that, finding himself puffing for breath after a quarter of an hour, he won't even persist till he gets his second wind, but will come back at once. Will he remark with genuine concern that his mind is sadly out of condition and that he really must do something to get it into order? Not he. It is a hundred to one that he will tranquilly accept the _status quo_, without shame and without very poignant regret. Do I make my meaning clear?

I say, without a _very poignant_ regret, because a certain vague regret is indubitably caused by realizing that one is handicapped by a mental inefficiency which might, without too much difficulty, be cured. That vague regret exudes like a vapor from the more cultivated section of the public. It is to be detected everywhere, and especially among people who are near the half-way house of life. They perceive the existence of immense quantities of knowledge, not the smallest particle of which will they ever make their own. They stroll forth from their orderly dwellings on a starlit night, and feel dimly the wonder of the heavens. But the still small voice is telling them that, though they have read in a newspaper that there are fifty thousand stars in the Pleiades, they cannot even point to the Pleiades in the sky. How they would like to grasp the significance of the nebular theory, the most overwhelming of all theories! And the years are passing; and there are twenty-four hours in every day, out of which they work only six or seven; and it needs only an impulse, an effort, a system, in order gradually to cure the mind of its slackness, to give "tone" to its muscles, and to enable it to grapple with the splendors of knowledge and sensation that await it! But the regret is not poignant enough. They do nothing. They go on doing nothing. It is as though they passed for ever along the length of an endless table filled with delicacies, and could not stretch out a hand to seize. Do I exaggerate? Is there not deep in the consciousness of most of us a mournful feeling that our minds are like the liver of the advertisement--sluggish, and that for the sluggishness of our minds there is the excuse neither of incompetence, nor of lack of time, nor of lack of opportunity, nor of lack of means?

Why does not some mental efficiency specialist come forward and show us how to make our minds do the work which our minds are certainly capable of doing? I do not mean a quack. All the physical efficiency specialists who advertise largely are not quacks. Some of them achieve very genuine results. If a course of treatment can be devised for the body, a course of treatment can be devised for the mind. Thus we might realize some of the ambitions which all of us cherish in regard to the utilization in our spare time of that magnificent machine which we allow to rust within our craniums. We have the desire to perfect ourselves, to round off our careers with the graces of knowledge and taste. How many people would not gladly undertake some branch of serious study, so that they might not die under the reproach of having lived and died without ever really having known anything about anything! It is not the absence of desire that prevents them. It is, first, the absence of will-power--not the will to begin, but the will to continue; and, second, a mental apparatus which is out of condition, "puffy," "weedy," through sheer neglect. The remedy, then, divides itself into two parts, the cultivation of will-power, and the getting into condition of the mental apparatus. And these two branches of the cure must be worked concurrently.

I am sure that the considerations which I have presented to you must have already presented themselves to tens of thousands of my readers, and that thousands must have attempted the cure. I doubt not that many have succeeded. I shall deem it a favour if those readers who have interested themselves in the question will communicate to me at once the result of their experience, whatever its outcome. I will make such use as I can of the letters I receive, and afterwards I will give my own experience.

THE REPLIES

The correspondence which I have received in answer to my
appeal shows that at any rate I did not overstate the case. There
is, among a vast mass of reflecting people in this country, a clear
consciousness of being mentally less than efficient, and a strong
(though ineffective) desire that such mental inefficiency should
cease to be. The desire is stronger than I had imagined, but it
does not seem to have led to much hitherto. And that "course of
treatment for the mind," by means of which we are to "realize
some of the ambitions which all of us cherish in regard to the
utilization in our spare time of the magnificent machine which
we allow to rust within our craniums"--that desiderated course
of treatment has not apparently been devised by anybody. The
Sandow of the brain has not yet loomed up above the horizon.
On the other hand, there appears to be a general expectancy that
I personally am going to play the role of the Sandow of the brain.
Vain thought!

I have been very much interested in the letters, some of which,
as a statement of the matter in question, are admirable. It is
perhaps not surprising that the best of them come from women-
-for (genius apart) woman is usually more touchingly lyrical
than man in the yearning for the ideal. The most enthusiastic of
all the letters I have received, however, is from a gentleman
whose notion is that we should be hypnotized into mental
efficiency. After advocating the establishment of "an institution
of practical psychology from whence there can be graduated fit
and proper people whose efforts would be in the direction of the
subconscious mental mechanism of the child or even the adult,"
this hypnotist proceeds: "Between the academician, whose
specialty is an inconsequential cobweb, the medical man who
has got it into his head that he is the logical foster-father for

121

psychonomical matters, and the blatant 'professor' who deals with monkey tricks on a few somnambules on the music-hall stage, you are allowing to go unrecognized one of the most potent factors of mental development." Am I? I have not the least idea what this gentleman means, but I can assure him that he is wrong. I can make more sense out of the remarks of another correspondent who, utterly despising the things of the mind, compares a certain class of young men to "a halfpenny bloater with the roe out," and asserts that he himself "got out of the groove" by dint of having to unload ten tons of coal in three hours and a half every day during several years. This is interesting and it is constructive, but it is just a little beside the point.

A lady, whose optimism is indicated by her pseudonym, "Esperance," puts her finger on the spot, or, rather, on one of the spots, in a very sensible letter. "It appears to me," she says, "that the great cause of mental inefficiency is lack of concentration, perhaps especially in the case of women. I can trace my chief failures to this cause. Concentration, is a talent. It may be in a measure cultivated, but it needs to be inborn.... The greater number of us are in a state of semi-slumber, with minds which are only exerted to one-half of their capability." I thoroughly agree that inability to concentrate is one of the chief symptoms of the mental machine being out of condition. "Esperance's" suggested cure is rather drastic. She says: "Perhaps one of the best cures for mental sedentariness is arithmetic, for there is nothing else which requires greater power of concentration." Perhaps arithmetic might be an effective cure, but it is not a practical cure, because no one, or scarcely any one, would practice it. I cannot imagine the plain man who, having a couple of hours to spare of a night, and having also the sincere desire but not the will-power to improve his taste and knowledge, would deliberately sit down and work sums by way of preliminary mental calisthenics. As Ibsen's puppet said: "People don't do these things." Why do they not? The answer is: Simply because they won't; simply because human nature will not run to it. "Esperance's" suggestion of learning poetry is slightly better.

Certainly the best letter I have had is from Miss H. D. She says: "This idea [to avoid the reproach of 'living and dying without ever really knowing anything about anything'] came to me of itself from somewhere when I was a small girl. And looking back I fancy that the thought itself spurred me to do something in this world, to get into line with people who did things--people who painted pictures, wrote books, built bridges, or did something beyond the ordinary. This only has seemed to me, all my life since, worthwhile." Here I must interject that such a statement is somewhat sweeping. In fact, it sweeps a whole lot of fine and legitimate ambitions straight into the rubbish heap of the Not-worth-while. I think the writer would wish to modify it. She continues: "And when the day comes in which I have not done some serious reading, however small the measure, or some writing ... or I have been too sad or dull to notice the brightness of color of the sun, of grass and flowers, of the sea, or the moonlight on the water, I think the day ill-spent. So I must think the _incentive_ to do a little each day beyond the ordinary towards the real culture of the mind, is the beginning of the cure of mental inefficiency." This is very ingenious and good. Further: "The day comes when the mental habit has become a part of our life, and we value mental work for the work's sake." But I am not sure about that. For myself, I have never valued work for its own sake, and I never shall. And I only value such mental work for the more full and more intense consciousness of being alive which it gives me.

Miss H. D.'s remedies are vague. As to lack of will-power, "the first step is to realize your weakness; the next step is to have ordinary shame that you are defective." I doubt, I gravely doubt, if these steps would lead to anything definite. Nor is this very helpful: "I would advise reading, observing, writing. I would advise the use of every sense and every faculty by which we at last learn the sacredness of life." This is begging the question. If people, by merely wishing to do so, could regularly and seriously read, observe, write, and use every faculty and sense, there would be very little mental inefficiency. I see that I shall be driven to construct a program out of my own bitter and ridiculous experiences.

THE CURE

"But tasks in hours of insight willed can be through hours of gloom fulfilled."

The above lines from Matthew Arnold are quoted by one of my very numerous correspondents to support a certain optimism in this matter of a systematic attempt to improve the mind. They form part of a beautiful and inspiring poem, but I gravely fear that they run counter to the vast mass of earthly experience. More often than not I have found that a task willed in some hour of insight can _not_ be fulfilled through hours of gloom. No, no, and no! To will is easy: it needs but the momentary bright contagion of a stronger spirit than one's own. To fulfil, morning after morning, or evening after evening, through months and years--this is the very dickens, and there is not one of my readers that will not agree with me. Yet such is the elastic quality of human nature that most of my correspondents are quite ready to ignore the sad fact and to demand at once: "what shall we will? Tell us what we must will." Some seem to think that they have solved the difficulty when they have advocated certain systems of memory and mind-training. Such systems may be in themselves useful or useless--the evidence furnished to me is contradictory--but were they perfect systems, a man cannot be intellectually born again merely by joining a memory-class. The best system depends utterly on the man's power of resolution. And what really counts is not the system, but the spirit in which the man handles it. Now, the proper spirit can only be induced by a careful consideration and realization of the man's conditions--the limitations of his temperament, the strength of adverse influences, and the lessons of his past.

Let me take an average case. Let me take your case, O man or woman of thirty, living in comfort, with some cares, and some responsibilities, and some pretty hard daily work, but not too much of any! The question of mental efficiency is in the air. It interests you. It touches you nearly. Your conscience tells you that your mind is less active and less informed than it might be. You suddenly spring up from the garden-seat, and you say to yourself that you will take your mind in hand and do something with it. Wait a moment. Be so good as to sink back into that garden-seat and clutch that tennis racket a little longer. You have had these "hours of insight" before, you know. You have not arrived at the age of thirty without having tried to carry out noble resolutions--and failed. What precautions are you going to take against failure this time? For your will is probably no stronger now than it was aforetime. You have admitted and accepted failure in the past. And no wound is more cruel to the spirit of resolve than that dealt by failure. You fancy the wound closed, but just at the critical moment it may reopen and mortally bleed you. What are your precautions? Have you thought of them? No. You have not.

I have not the pleasure of your acquaintance. But I know you because I know myself. Your failure in the past was due to one or more of three causes. And the first was that you undertook too much at the beginning. You started off with a magnificent program. You are something of an expert in physical exercises--

you would be ashamed not to be, in these physical days--and so you would never attempt a hurdle race or an uninterrupted hour's club-whirling without some preparation. The analogy between the body and the mind ought to have struck you. _This_ time, please do not form an elaborate program. Do not form any program. Simply content yourself with a preliminary canter, a ridiculously easy preliminary canter. For example (and I give this merely as an example), you might say to yourself: "Within one month from this date I will read twice Herbert Spencer's little book on 'Education'--sixpence--and will make notes in pencil inside the back cover of the things that particularly strike me." You remark that that is nothing, that you can do it "on your head," and so on. Well, do it. When it is done you will at any rate possess the satisfaction of having resolved to do something and having done it. Your mind will have gained tone and healthy pride. You will be even justified in setting yourself some kind of a simple program to extend over three months. And you will have acquired some general principles by the light of which to construct the program. But best of all, you will have avoided failure, that dangerous wound.

The second possible cause of previous failure was the disintegrating effect on the will-power of the ironic, superior smile of friends. Whenever a man "turns over a new leaf" he has this inane giggle to face. The drunkard may be less ashamed of getting drunk than of breaking to a crony the news that he has signed the pledge. Strange, but true! And human nature must be counted with. Of course, on a few stern spirits the effect of that smile is merely to harden the resolution. But on the majority its influence is deleterious. Therefore don't go and nail your flag to the mast. Don't raise any flag. Say nothing. Work as unobtrusively as you can. When you have won a battle or two you can begin to wave the banner, and then you will find that

that miserable, pitiful, ironic, superior smile will die away ere it is born.

The third possible cause was that you did not rearrange your day. Idler and time-waster though you have been, still you had done _something_ during the twenty-four hours. You went to work with a kind of dim idea that there were twenty-six hours in every day. _Something large and definite has to be dropped._ Some space in the rank jungle of the day has to be cleared and swept up for the new operations. Robbing yourself of sleep won't help you, nor trying to "squeeze in" a time for study between two other times. Use the knife, and use it freely. If you mean to read or think half an hour a day, arrange for an hour. A hundred per cent. margin is not too much for a beginner. Do you ask me where the knife is to be used? I should say that in nine cases out of ten the rites of the cult of the body might be abbreviated. I recently spent a week-end in a London suburb, and I was staggered by the wholesale attention given to physical recreation in all its forms. It was a gigantic debauch of the muscles on every side. It shocked me. "Poor withering mind!" I thought. "Cricket, and football, and boating, and golf, and tennis have their 'seasons,' but not thou!" These considerations are general and prefatory. Now I must come to detail.

MENTAL CALISTHENICS

I have dealt with the state of mind in which one should begin a serious effort towards mental efficiency, and also with the probable causes of failure in previous efforts. We come now to what I may call the calisthenics of the business, exercises which may be roughly compared to the technical exercises necessary in learning to play a musical instrument. It is curious that a person studying a musical instrument will have no false shame whatever in doing mere exercises for the fingers and wrists while a person who is trying to get his mind into order will almost certainly experience a false shame in going through performances which are undoubtedly good for him. Herein lies one of the great obstacles to mental efficiency. Tell a man that he should join a memory class, and he will hum and haw, and say, as I have already remarked, that memory isn't everything; and, in short, he won't join the memory class, partly from indolence, I grant, but more from false shame. (Is not this true?) He will even hesitate about learning things by heart. Yet there are few mental exercises better than learning great poetry or prose by heart. Twenty lines a week for six months: what a "cure" for debility! The chief, but not the only, merit of learning by heart as an exercise is that it compels the mind to concentrate. And the most important preliminary to self-development is the faculty of concentrating at will. Another excellent exercise is to read a page of no-matter-what, and then immediately to write down--in one's own words or in the author's--one's full recollection of it. A quarter of an hour a day! No more! And it works like magic.

This brings me to the department of writing. I am a writer by profession; but I do not think I have any prejudices in favor of the exercise of writing. Indeed, I say to myself every morning that if there is one exercise in the world which I hate, it is the exercise of writing. But I must assert that in my opinion the exercise of writing is an indispensable part of any genuine effort towards mental efficiency. I don't care much what you write, so long as you compose sentences and achieve continuity. There are forty ways of writing in an unprofessional manner, and they are all good. You may keep "a full diary," as Mr. Arthur Christopher Benson says he does. This is one of the least good ways. Diaries, save in experienced hands like those of Mr. Benson, are apt to get themselves done with the very minimum of mental effort. They also tend to an exaggeration of egotism, and if they are left lying about they tend to strife. Further, one never knows when one may not be compelled to produce them in a court of law. A journal is better. Do not ask me to define the difference between a journal and a diary. I will not and I cannot. It is a difference that one feels instinctively. A diary treats exclusively of one's self and one's doings; a journal roams wider, and notes whatever one has observed of interest. A diary relates that one had lobster mayonnaise for dinner and rose the next morning with a headache, doubtless attributable to mental strain. A journal relates that Mrs. ----, whom one took into dinner, had brown eyes, and an agreeable trick of throwing back her head after asking a question, and gives her account of her husband's strange adventures in Colorado, etc. A diary is

All I, I, I, I, itself I

(to quote a line of the transcendental poetry of Mary Baker G. Eddy). A journal is the large spectacle of life. A journal may be special or general. I know a man who keeps a journal of all cases of current superstition which he actually encounters. He began it without the slightest suspicion that he was beginning a document of astounding interest and real scientific value; but such was the fact. In default of a diary or a journal, one may write essays (provided one has the moral courage); or one may simply make notes on the book one reads. Or one may construct anthologies of passages which have made an individual and particular appeal to one's tastes. Anthology construction is one of the pleasantest hobbies that a person who is not mad about golf and bridge--that is to say, a thinking person--can possibly have; and I recommend it to those who, discreetly mistrusting their power to keep up a fast pace from start to finish, are anxious to begin their intellectual course gently and mildly. In any event, writing--the act of writing--is vital to almost any scheme. I would say it was vital to every scheme, without exception, were I not sure that some kind correspondent would instantly point out a scheme to which writing was obviously not vital.

After writing comes thinking. (The sequence may be considered odd, but I adhere to it.) In this connexion I cannot do better than quote an admirable letter which I have received from a correspondent who wishes to be known only as "An Oxford Lecturer." The italics (except the last) are mine, not his. He says: "Till a man has got his physical brain completely under his control--_suppressing its too-great receptivity, its tendencies to reproduce idly the thoughts of others, and to be swayed by every passing gust of emotion_--I hold that he cannot do a tenth part of the work that he would then be able to perform with little or no effort. Moreover, work apart, he has not entered upon his kingdom, and unlimited possibilities of future development are barred to him. Mental efficiency can be gained by constant practice in meditation--i.e., by concentrating the mind, say, for but ten minutes daily, but with absolute regularity, on some of the highest thoughts of which it is capable. Failures will be frequent, but they must be regarded with simple indifference and dogged perseverance in the path chosen. If that path be followed _without intermission_ even for a few weeks the results will speak for themselves." I thoroughly agree with what this correspondent says, and am obliged to him for having so ably stated the case. But I regard such a practice of meditation as he indicates as being rather an "advanced" exercise for a beginner. After the beginner has got under way, and gained a little confidence in his strength of purpose, and acquired the skill to define his thoughts sufficiently to write them down--then it would be time enough, in my view, to undertake what "An Oxford Lecturer" suggests. By the way, he highly recommends Mrs. Annie Besant's book, _Thought Power: Its Control and Culture_. He says that it treats the subject with scientific clearness, and gives a practical method of training the mind, I endorse the latter part of the statement.

So much for the more or less technical processes of stirring the mind from its sloth and making it exactly obedient to the aspirations of the soul. And here I close. Numerous correspondents have asked me to outline a course of reading for them. In other words, they have asked me to particularize for them the aspirations of their souls. My subject, however, was not self-development, my subject was mental efficiency as a means to self-development. Of course, one can only acquire mental efficiency in the actual effort of self-development. But I was concerned, not with the choice of route; rather with the manner of following the route. You say to me that I am busying myself with the best method of walking, and refusing to discuss where to go. Precisely. One man cannot tell another man where the other man wants to go.

If he can't himself decide on a goal he may as well curl up and expire, for the root of the matter is not in him. I will content myself with pointing out that the entire universe is open for inspection. Too many people fancy that self-development means literature. They associate the higher life with an intimate knowledge of the life of Charlotte Bronte, or the order of the plays of Shakespeare. The higher life may just as well be butterflies, or funeral customs, or county boundaries, or street names, or mosses, or stars, or slugs, as Charlotte Bronte or Shakespeare. Choose what interests you. Lots of finely-organized, mentally-efficient persons can't read Shakespeare at any price, and if you asked them who was the author of "The Tenant of Wildfell Hall" they might proudly answer Emily Bronte, if they didn't say they never heard of it. An accurate knowledge of any subject, coupled with a carefully nurtured sense of the relativity of that subject to other subjects, implies an enormous self-development. With this hint I conclude.

Chapter II

Expressing One's Individuality

A most curious and useful thing to realize is that one never knows the impression one is creating on other people. One may often guess pretty accurately whether it is good, bad, or indifferent--some people render it unnecessary for one to guess, they practically inform one--but that is not what I mean. I mean much more than that. I mean that one has one's self no mental picture corresponding to the mental picture which one's personality leaves in the minds of one's friends. Has it ever struck you that there is a mysterious individual going around, walking the streets, calling at houses for tea, chatting, laughing, grumbling, arguing, and that all your friends know him and have long since added him up and come to a definite conclusion about him--without saying more than a chance, cautious word to you; and that that person is _you_? Supposing that _you_ came into a drawing-room where you were having tea, do you think you would recognize yourself as an individuality? I think not. You would be apt to say to yourself, as guests do when disturbed in drawing-rooms by other guests: "Who's this chap? Seems rather queer, I hope he won't be a bore." And your first telling would be slightly hostile. Why, even when you meet yourself in an unsuspected mirror in the very clothes that you have put on that very day and that you know by heart, you are almost always shocked by the realization that you are you. And now and then, when you have gone to the glass to arrange your hair in the full sobriety of early morning, have you not looked on an absolute stranger, and has not that stranger piqued your curiosity? And if it is thus with precise external details of form, color, and movement, what may it not be with the vague complex effect of the mental and moral individuality?

A man honestly tries to make a good impression. What is the result? The result merely is that his friends, in the privacy of their minds, set him down as a man who tries to make a good impression. If much depends on the result of a single interview, or a couple of interviews, a man may conceivably force another to accept an impression of himself which he would like to convey. But if the receiver of the impression is to have time at his disposal, then the giver of the impression may just as well sit down and put his hands in his pockets, for nothing that he can do will modify or influence in any way the impression that he will ultimately give. The real impress is, in the end, given unconsciously, not consciously; and further, it is received unconsciously, not consciously. It depends partly on both persons. And it is immutably fixed beforehand. There can be no final deception. Take the extreme case, that of the mother and her son. One hears that the son hoodwinks his mother. Not he! If he is cruel, neglectful, overbearing, she is perfectly aware of it. He does not deceive her, and she does not deceive herself. I have often thought: If a son could look into a mother's heart, what an eye-opener he would have! "What!" he would cry. "This cold, impartial judgment, this keen vision for my faults, this implacable memory of little slights, and injustices, and callousnesses committed long ago, in the breast of my mother!" Yes, my friend, in the breast of your mother. The only difference between your mother and another person is that she takes you as you are, and loves you for what you are. She isn't blind: do not imagine it.

The marvel is, not that people are such bad judges of character, but that they are such good judges, especially of what I may call fundamental character. The wiliest person cannot forever conceal his fundamental character from the simplest. And people are very stern judges, too. Think of your best friends--are you oblivious of their defects? On the contrary, you are perhaps too conscious of them. When you summon them before your mind's eye, it is no ideal creation that you see. When you meet them and talk to them you are constantly making reservations in their disfavor--unless, of course, you happen to be a schoolgirl gushing over like a fountain with enthusiasm. It is well, when one is judging a friend, to remember that he is judging you with the same godlike and superior impartiality. It is well to grasp the fact that you are going through life under the scrutiny of a band of acquaintances who are subject to very few illusions about you, whose views of you are, indeed, apt to be harsh and even cruel. Above all it is advisable to comprehend thoroughly that the things in your individuality which annoy your friends most are the things of which you are completely unconscious. It is not until years have passed that one begins to be able to form a dim idea of what one has looked like to one's friends. At forty one goes back ten years, and one says sadly, but with a certain amusement: "I must have been pretty blatant then. I can see how I must have exasperated 'em. And yet I hadn't the faintest notion of it at the time. My intentions were of the best. Only I didn't know enough." And one recollects some particularly crude action, and kicks one's self.... Yes, that is all very well; and the enlightenment which has come with increasing age is exceedingly satisfactory. But you are forty now. What shall you be saying of yourself at fifty? Such reflections foster humility, and they foster also a reluctance, which it is impossible to praise too highly, to tread on other people's toes.

A moment ago I used the phrase "fundamental character." It is a reminiscence of Stevenson's phrase "fundamental decency." And it is the final test by which one judges one's friends. "After all, he's a decent fellow." We must be able to use that formula concerning our friends. Kindliness of heart is not the greatest of human qualities--and its general effect on the progress of the world is not entirely beneficent--but it is the greatest of human qualities in friendship. It is the least dispensable quality. We come back to it with relief from more brilliant qualities. And it has the great advantage of always going with a broad mind. Narrow-minded people are never kind-hearted. You may be inclined to dispute this statement: please think it over; I am inclined to uphold it.

We can forgive the absence of any quality except kindliness of heart. And when a man lacks that, we blame him, we will not forgive him. This is, of course, scandalous. A man is born as he is born. And he can as easily add a cubit to his stature as add kindliness to his heart. The feat never has been done, and never will be done. And yet we blame those who have not kindliness. We have the incredible, insufferable, and odious audacity to blame them. We think of them as though they had nothing to do but go into a shop and buy kindliness. I hear you say that kindliness of heart can be "cultivated." Well, I hate to have even the appearance of contradicting you, but it can only be cultivated in the botanical sense. You can't cultivate violets on a nettle. A philosopher has enjoined us to suffer fools gladly. He had more usefully enjoined us to suffer ill-natured persons gladly.... I see that in a fit of absentmindedness I have strayed into the pulpit. I descend.

Chapter III

Breaking with the Past

On that dark morning we woke up, and it instantly occurred to us--or at any rate to those of us who have preserved some of our illusions and our "naiveté" that we had something to be cheerful about, some cause for a gay and strenuous vivacity; and then we remembered that it was New Year's Day, and there were those Resolutions to put into force! Of course, we all smile in a superior manner at the very mention of New Year's Resolutions; we pretend they are toys for children, and that we have long since ceased to regard them seriously as a possible aid to conduct. But we are such deceivers, such miserable, moral cowards, in such terror of appearing naive that I for one am not to be taken in by that smile and that pretense. The individual who scoffs at New Year's Resolutions resembles the woman who says she doesn't look under the bed at nights; the truth is not in him, and in the very moment of his lying, could his cranium suddenly become transparent, we should see Resolutions burning brightly in his brain like lamps in Trafalgar Square. Of this I am convinced, that nineteen-twentieths of us got out of bed that morning animated by that special feeling of gay and strenuous vivacity which Resolutions alone can produce. And nineteen-twentieths of us were also conscious of a high virtue, forgetting that it is not the making of Resolutions, but the keeping of them, which renders pardonable the consciousness of virtue.

And at this hour, while the activity of the Resolution is yet in full blast, I would wish to insist on the truism, obvious perhaps, but apt to be overlooked, that a man cannot go forward and stand still at the same time. Just as moralists have often animadverted upon the tendency to live in the future, so I would animadvert upon the tendency to live in the past. Because all around me I see men carefully tying themselves with an unbreakable rope to an immovable post at the bottom of a hill and then struggling to climb the hill. If there is one Resolution more important than another it is the Resolution to break with the past. If life is not a continual denial of the past, then it is nothing. This may seem a hard and callous doctrine, but you know there are aspects of common sense which decidedly are hard and callous. And one finds constantly in plain common-sense persons (O rare and select band!) a surprising quality of ruthlessness mingled with softer traits. Have you not noticed it? The past is absolutely intractable. One can't do anything with it. And an exaggerated attention to it is like an exaggerated attention to sepulchers--a sign of barbarism. Moreover, the past is usually the enemy of cheerfulness, and cheerfulness is a most precious attainment.

Personally, I could even go so far as to exhibit hostility towards grief, and a marked hostility towards remorse--two states of mind which feed on the past instead of on the present. Remorse, which is not the same thing as repentance, serves no purpose that I have ever been able to discover. What one has done, one has done, and there's an end of it. As a great prelate unforgettably said, "Things are what they are, and the consequences of them will be what they will be. Why, then, attempt to deceive ourselves"--that remorse for wickedness is a useful and praiseworthy exercise? Much better to forget. As a matter of fact, people "indulge" in remorse; it is a somewhat vicious form of spiritual pleasure. Grief, of course, is different, and it must be handled with delicate consideration.

Nevertheless, when I see, as one does see, a man or a woman dedicating existence to sorrow for the loss of a beloved creature, and the world tacitly applauding, my feeling is certainly inimical. To my idea, that man or woman is not honoring, but dishonoring, the memory of the departed; society suffers, the individual suffers, and no earthly or heavenly good is achieved. Grief is of the past; it mars the present; it is a form of indulgence, and it ought to be bridled much more than it often is. The human heart is so large that mere remembrance should not be allowed to tyrannize over every part of it.

But cases of remorse and absorbing grief are comparatively rare. What is not rare is that misguided loyalty to the past which dominates the lives of so many of us. I do not speak of leading principles, which are not likely to incommode us by changing; I speak of secondary yet still important things. We will not do so-and-so because we have never done it--as if that was a reason! Or we have always done so-and-so, therefore we must always do it--as if _that_ was logic! This disposition to an irrational Toryism is curiously discoverable in advanced Radicals, and it will show itself in the veriest trifles. I remember such a man whose wife objected to his form of hat (not that I would call so crowning an affair as a hat a trifle!). "My dear," he protested, "I have always worn this sort of hat. It may not suit me, but it is absolutely impossible for me to alter it now." However, she took him by means of an omnibus to a hat shop and bought him another hat and put it on his head, and made a present of the old one to the shop assistant, and marched him out of the shop. "There!" she said, "you see how impossible it is." This is a parable. And I will not insult your intelligence by applying it.

The faculty that we chiefly need when we are in the resolution-making mood is the faculty of imagination, the faculty of looking at our lives as though we had never looked at them before--freshly, with a new eye. Supposing that you had been born mature and full of experience, and that yesterday had been the first day of your life, you would regard it to-day as an experiment, you would challenge each act in it, and you would probably arrange to-morrow in a manner that showed a healthy disrespect for yesterday. You certainly would not say: "I have done so-and-so once, therefore I must keep on doing it." The past is never more than an experiment. A genuine appreciation of this fact will make our new Resolutions more valuable and drastic than they usually are. I have a dim notion that the most useful Resolution for most of us would be to break quite fifty per cent of all the vows we have ever made. "*Do not accustom yourself to enchain your _volatility_ with vows.... Take this warning; it is of great importance.*" (The wisdom is Johnson's, but I flatter myself on the italics.)

Chapter IV

Settling Down in Life

The other day a well-known English novelist asked me how old I thought she was, _really_. "Well," I said to myself, "since she has asked for it, she shall have it; I will be as true to life as her novels." So I replied audaciously: "Thirty-eight." I fancied I was erring if at all, on the side of "really," and I trembled. She laughed triumphantly. "I am forty-three," she said. The incident might have passed off entirely to my satisfaction had she not proceeded: "And now tell me how old _you_ are." That was like a woman. Women imagine that men have no reticences, no pretty little vanities. What an error! Of course I could not be beaten in candor by a woman. I had to offer myself a burnt sacrifice to her curiosity, and I did it, bravely but not unflinchingly. And then afterwards the fact of my age remained with me, worried me, obsessed me. I saw more clearly than ever before that age was telling on me. I could not be blind to the deliberation of my movements in climbing stairs and in dressing. Once upon a time the majority of persons I met in the street seemed much older than myself. It is different now. The change has come unperceived. There is a generation younger than mine that smokes cigars and falls in love. Astounding! Once I could play left-wing forward for an hour and a half without dropping down dead. Once I could swim a hundred and fifty feet submerged at the bottom of a swimming-bath. Incredible! Simply incredible!... Can it be that I have already lived?

And lo! I, at the age of nearly forty, am putting to myself the old questions concerning the intrinsic value of life, the fundamentally important questions: What have I got out of it? What am I likely to get out of it? In a word, what's it worth? If a man can ask himself a question more momentous, radical, and critical than these questions, I would like to know what it is. Innumerable philosophers have tried to answer these questions in a general way for the average individual, and possibly they have succeeded pretty well. Possibly I might derive benefit from a perusal of their answers. But do you suppose I am going to read them? Not I! Do you suppose that I can recall the wisdom that I happen already to have read? Not I! My mind is a perfect blank at this moment in regard to the wisdom of others on the essential question. Strange, is it not? But quite a common experience, I believe. Besides, I don't actually care two pence what any other philosopher has replied to my question. In this, each man must be his own philosopher. There is an instinct in the profound egoism of human nature which prevents us from accepting such ready-made answers. What is it to us what Plato thought? Nothing. And thus the question remains ever new, and ever unanswered, and ever of dramatic interest. The singular, the highly singular thing is--and here I arrive at my point--that so few people put the question to themselves in time, that so many put it too late, or even die without putting it.

I am firmly convinced that an immense proportion of my instructed fellow-creatures do not merely omit to strike the balance-sheet of their lives, they omit even the preliminary operation of taking stock. They go on, and on, and on, buying and selling they know not what, at unascertained prices, dropping money into the till and taking it out. They don't know what goods are in the shop, nor what amount is in the till, but they have a clear impression that the living-room behind the shop is by no means as luxurious and as well-ventilated as they would like it to be. And the years pass, and that beautiful furniture and that system of ventilation are not achieved. And then one day they die, and friends come to the funeral and remark: "Dear me! How stuffy this room is, and the shop's practically full of trash!" Or, some little time before they are dead, they stay later than usual in the shop one evening, and make up their minds to take stock and count the till, and the disillusion lays them low, and they struggle into the living-room and murmur: "I shall never have that beautiful furniture, and I shall never have that system of ventilation. If I had known earlier, I would have at least got a few inexpensive cushions to go on with, and I would have put my fist through a pane in the window. But it's too late now. I'm used to Windsor chairs, and I should feel the draught horribly."

If I were a preacher, and if I hadn't got more than enough to do in minding my own affairs, and if I could look any one in the face and deny that I too had pursued for nearly forty years the great British policy of muddling through and hoping for the best--in short, if things were not what they are, I would hire the Alhambra Theatre or Exeter Hall of a Sunday night--preferably the Alhambra, because more people would come to my entertainment--and I would invite all men and women over twenty-six. I would supply the seething crowd with what they desired in the way of bodily refreshment (except spirits--I would draw the line at poisons), and having got them and myself into a nice amiable expansive frame of mind, I would thus address them--of course in ringing eloquence that John Bright might have envied:

Men and women (I would say), companions in the universal pastime of hiding one's head in the sand,--I am about to impart to you the very essence of human wisdom. It is not abstract. It is a principle of daily application, affecting the daily round in its entirety, from the straphanging on the District Railway in the morning to the straphanging on the District Railway the next morning. Beware of hope, and beware of ambition! Each is excellently tonic, like German competition, in moderation. But all of you are suffering from self-indulgence in the first, and very many of you are ruining your constitutions with the second. Be it known unto you, my dear men and women, that existence rightly considered is a fair compromise between two instincts-- the instinct of hoping one day to live, and the instinct to live here and now. In most of you the first instinct has simply got the other by the throat and is throttling it. Prepare to live by all means, but for heaven's sake do not forget to live. You will never have a better chance than you have at present. You may think you will have, but you are mistaken. Pardon this bluntness. Surely you are not so naive as to imagine that the road on the other side of that hill there is more beautiful than the piece you are now traversing! Hopes are never realized; for in the act of realization they become something else. Ambitions may be attained, but ambitions attained are rather like burnt coal, ninety per cent of the heat generated has gone up the chimney instead of into the room. Nevertheless, indulge in hopes and ambitions, which, though deceiving, are agreeable deceptions; let them cheat you a little, a lot. But do not let them cheat you too much. This that you are living now is life itself--it is much more life itself than that which you will be living twenty years hence. Grasp that truth. Dwell on it. Absorb it. Let it influence your conduct, to the end that neither the present nor the future be neglected. You search for happiness? Happiness is chiefly a matter of temperament. It is exceedingly improbable that you will by struggling gain more happiness than you already possess. In fine, settle down at once into "life". (Loud cheers.)

The cheers would of course be for the refreshments.

There is no doubt that the mass of the audience would consider that I had missed my vocation, and ought to have been a caterer instead of a preacher. But, once started, I would not be discouraged. I would keep on, Sunday night after Sunday night. Our leading advertisers have richly proved that the public will believe anything if they are told of it often enough. I would practice iteration, always with refreshments. In the result, it would dawn upon the corporate mind that there was some glimmering of sense in my doctrine, and people would at last begin to perceive the folly of neglecting to savor the present, the folly of assuming that the future can be essentially different from the present, the fatuity of dying before they have begun to live.

Chapter V

Marriage

THE DUTY OF IT

Every now and then it becomes necessary to deal faithfully with that immortal type of person, the praiser of the past at the expense of the present. I will not quote Horace, as by all the traditions of letters I ought to do, because Horace, like the incurable trimmer that he was, "hedged" on this question; and I do not admire him much either. The praiser of the past has been very rife lately. He has told us that pauperism and lunacy are mightily increasing, and though the exact opposite has been proved to be the case and he has apologized, he will have forgotten the correction in a few months, and will break out again into renewed lamentation. He has told us that we are physically deteriorating, and in such awful tones that we have shuddered, and many of us have believed. And considering that the death-rate is decreasing, that slums are decreasing, that disease is decreasing, that the agricultural laborer eats more than ever he did, our credence does not do much credit to our reasoning powers, does it? Of course, there is that terrible "influx" into the towns, but I for one should be much interested to know wherein the existence of the rustic in times past was healthier than the existence of the town-dwellers of to-day. The personal appearance of agricultural veterans does not help me; they resemble starved 'bus-drivers twisted out of shape by lightning.

But the _piece de resistance_ of the praiser of the past is now marriage, with discreet hints about the birth-rate. The praiser of the past is going to have a magnificent time with the subject of marriage. The first moanings of the tempest have already been heard. Bishops have looked askance at the birth-rate, and have mentioned their displeasure. The matter is serious. As the phrase goes, "it strikes at the root." We are marrying later, my friends. Some of us, in the hurry and pre-occupation of business, are quite forgetting to marry. It is the duty of the citizen to marry and have children, and we are neglecting our duty, we are growing selfish! No longer are produced the glorious "quiverfuls" of old times! Our fathers married at twenty; we marry at thirty-five. Why? Because a gross and enervating luxury has overtaken us. What will become of England if this continues? There will be no England! Hence we must look to it! And so on, in the same strain.

I should like to ask all those who have raised and will raise such outcries. Have you read "X"? Now, the book that I refer to as "X" is a mysterious work, written rather more than a hundred years ago by an English curate. It is a classic of English science; indeed, it is one of the great scientific books of the world. It has immensely influenced all the scientific thought of the nineteenth century, especially Darwin's. Mr. H.G. Wells, as cited in "Chambers's Cyclopaedia of English Literature," describes it as "the most 'shattering' book that ever has or will be written." If I may make a personal reference, I would say that it affected me more deeply than any other scientific book that I have read. Although it is perfectly easy to understand, and free from the slightest technicality, it is the most misunderstood book in English literature, simply because it is _not_ read. The current notion about it is utterly false. It might be a powerful instrument of education, general and sociological, but publishers will not reprint it--at least, they do not. And yet it is forty times more interesting and four hundred times more educational than Gilbert White's remarks on the birds of Selborne. I will leave you to guess what "X" is, but I do not offer a prize for the solution of a problem which a vast number of my readers will certainly solve at once.

If those who are worrying themselves about the change in our system of marriage would read "X," they would probably cease from worrying. For they would perceive that they had been putting the cart before the horse; that they had elevated to the dignity of fundamental principles certain average rules of conduct which had sprung solely from certain average instincts in certain average conditions, and that they were now frightened because, the conditions having changed, the rules of conduct had changed with them. One of the truths that "X" makes clear is that conduct conforms to conditions, and not conditions to conduct.

The payment of taxes is a duty which the citizen owes to the state. Marriage, with the begetting of children, is not a duty which the citizen owes to the state. Marriage, with its consequences, is a matter of personal inclination and convenience. It never has been anything else, and it never will be anything else. How could it be otherwise? If a man goes against inclination and convenience in a matter where inclination is "of the essence of the contract," he merely presents the state with a discontented citizen (if not two) in exchange for a contented one! The happiness of the state is the sum of the happiness of all its citizens; to decrease one's own happiness, then, is a singular way of doing one's duty to the state! Do you imagine that when people married early and much they did so from a sense of duty to the state--a sense of duty which our "modern luxury" has weakened? I imagine they married simply because it suited 'em. They married from sheer selfishness, as all decent people do marry. And do those who clatter about the duty of marriage kiss the girls of their hearts with an eye to the general welfare? I can fancy them saying, "My angel, I love you--from a sense of duty to the state. Let us rear innumerable progeny--from a sense of duty to the state." How charmed the girls would be!

If the marrying age changes, if the birth-rate shows a sympathetic tendency to follow the death-rate (as it must--see "X"), no one need be alarmed. Elementary principles of right and wrong are not trembling on their bases. The human conscience is not silenced. The nation is not going to the dogs. Conduct is adjusting itself to new conditions, and that is all. We may not be able to see exactly _how_ conditions are changing; that is a detail; our descendants will see exactly; meanwhile the change in our conduct affords us some clew. And although certain nervous persons do get alarmed, and do preach, and do "take measures," the rest of us may remain placid in the sure faith that "measures" will avail nothing whatever. If there are two things set high above legislation, "movements," crusades, and preaching, one is the marrying age and the other is the birth-rate. For there the supreme instinct comes along and stamps ruthlessly on all insincere reasonings and sham altruisms; stamps on everything, in fact, and blandly remarks: "I shall suit my own convenience, and no one but Nature herself (with a big, big N) shall talk to _me_. Don't pester me with Right and Wrong. I _am_ Right and Wrong...." Having thus attempted to clear the ground a little of fudge, I propose next to offer a few simple remarks on marriage.

THE ADVENTURE OF IT

Having endeavored to show that men do not, and should not, marry from a sense of duty to the state or to mankind, but simply and solely from an egoistic inclination to marry, I now proceed to the individual case of the man who is "in a position to marry" and whose affections are not employed. Of course, if he has fallen in love, unless he happens to be a person of extremely powerful will, he will not weigh the pros and cons of marriage; he will merely marry, and forty thousand cons will not prevent him. And he will be absolutely right and justified, just as the straw as it rushes down the current is absolutely right and justified. But the privilege of falling in love is not given to everybody, and the inestimable privilege of falling deeply in love is given to few. However, the man whom circumstances permit to marry but who is not in love, or is only slightly amorous, will still think of marriage. How will he think of it?

I will tell you. In the first place, if he has reached the age of thirty unscathed by Aphrodite, he will reflect that that peculiar feeling of romantic expectation with which he gets up every morning would cease to exist after marriage--and it is a highly agreeable feeling! In its stead, in moments of depression, he would have the feeling of having done something irremediable, of having definitely closed an avenue for the outlet of his individuality. (Kindly remember that I am not describing what this human man ought to think. I am describing what he does think.) In the second place, he will reflect that, after marriage, he could no longer expect the charming welcomes which bachelors so often receive from women; he would be "done with" as a possibility, and he does not relish the prospect of being done with as a possibility. Such considerations, all connected more or less with the loss of "freedom" (oh, mysterious and thrilling word!), will affect his theoretical attitude. And be it known that even the freedom to be lonely and melancholy is still freedom.

Other ideas will suggest themselves. One morning while brushing his hair he will see a gray hair, and, however young he may be, the anticipation of old age will come to him. A solitary old age! A senility dependent for its social and domestic requirements on condescending nephews and nieces, or even more distant relations! Awful! Unthinkable! And his first movement, especially if he has read that terrible novel, "Fort comme la Mort," of De Maupassant, is to rush out into the street and propose to the first girl he encounters, in order to avoid this dreadful nightmare of a solitary old age. But before he has got as far as the doorstep he reflects further. Suppose he marries, and after twenty years his wife dies and leaves him a widower! He will still have a solitary old age, and a vastly more tragical one than if he had remained single. Marriage is not, therefore, a sure remedy for a solitary old age; it may intensify the evil. Children? But suppose he doesn't have any children! Suppose, there being children, they die--what anguish! Suppose merely that they are seriously ill and recover--what an ageing experience! Suppose they prove a disappointment--what endless regret! Suppose they "turn out badly" (children do)--what shame! Suppose he finally becomes dependent upon the grudging kindness of an ungrateful child--what a supreme humiliation! All these things are occurring constantly everywhere. Suppose his wife, having loved him, ceased to love him, or suppose he ceased to love his wife! "Ces choses ne se commandent pas", these things do not command themselves. Personally, I should estimate that in not one per cent even of romantic marriages are the husband and wife capable of _passion_ for each other after three years. So brief is the violence of love! In perhaps thirty-three per cent passion settles down into a tranquil affection--which is ideal. In fifty per cent it sinks into sheer indifference, and one becomes used to one's wife or one's husband as to one's other habits. And in the remaining sixteen per cent it develops into dislike or detestation. Do you think my percentages are wrong, you who have been married a long time and know what the world is? Well, you may modify them a little--you won't want to modify them much.

The risk of finding one's self ultimately among the sixteen per cent can be avoided by the simple expedient of not marrying. And by the same expedient the other risks can be avoided, together with yet others that I have not mentioned. It is entirely obvious, then (in fact, I beg pardon for mentioning it), that the attitude towards marriage of the heart-free bachelor must be at best a highly cautious attitude. He knows he is already in the frying-pan (none knows better), but, considering the propinquity of the fire, he doubts whether he had not better stay where he is. His life will be calmer, more like that of a hibernating snake; his sensibilities will be dulled; but the chances of poignant suffering will be very materially reduced.

So that the bachelor in a position to marry but not in love will assuredly decide in theory against marriage--that is to say, if he is timid, if he prefers frying-pans, if he is lacking in initiative, if he has the soul of a rat, if he wants to live as little as possible, if he hates his kind, if his egoism is of the miserable sort that dares not mingle with another's. But if he has been more happily gifted he will decide that the magnificent adventure is worth plunging into; the ineradicable and fine gambling instinct in him will urge him to take, at the first chance, a ticket in the only lottery permitted by the British Government. Because, after all, the mutual sense of ownership felt by the normal husband and the normal wife is something unique, something the like of which cannot be obtained without marriage. I saw a man and a woman at a sale the other day; I was too far off to hear them, but I could perceive they were having a most lively argument-- perhaps it was only about initials on pillowcases; they were _absorbed_ in themselves; the world did not exist for them. And I thought: "What miraculous exquisite Force is it that brings together that strange, somber, laconic organism in a silk hat and a loose, black overcoat, and that strange, bright, vivacious, querulous, irrational organism in brilliant fur and feathers?"

And when they moved away the most interesting phenomenon in the universe moved away. And I thought: "Just as no beer is bad, but some beer is better than other beer, so no marriage is bad." The chief reward of marriage is something which marriage is bound to give--companionship whose mysterious _interestingness_ nothing can stale. A man may hate his wife so that she can't thread a needle without annoying him, but when he dies, or she dies, he will say: "Well, _I was interested_." And one always is. Said a bachelor of forty-six to me the other night: "Anything is better than the void."

THE TWO WAYS OF IT

Sabine and other summary methods of marrying being now abandoned by all nice people, there remain two broad general ways. The first is the English way. We let nature take her course. We give heed to the heart's cry. When, amid the hazards and accidents of the world, two souls "find each other," we rejoice. Our instinctive wish is that they shall marry, if the matter can anyhow be arranged. We frankly recognize the claim of romance in life, and we are prepared to make sacrifices to it. We see a young couple at the altar; they are in love. Good! They are poor. So much the worse! But nevertheless we feel that love will pull them through. The revolting French system of bargain and barter is the one thing that we can neither comprehend nor pardon in the customs of our great neighbors. We endeavor to be polite about that system; we simply cannot. It shocks our finest, tenderest feelings. It is so obviously contrary to nature.

The second is the French way, just alluded to as bargain and barter. Now, if there is one thing a Frenchman can neither comprehend nor pardon in the customs of a race so marvelously practical and sagacious as ourselves, it is the English marriage system. He endeavors to be polite about it, and he succeeds. But it shocks his finest, tenderest feelings. He admits that it is in accordance with nature; but he is apt to argue that the whole progress of civilization has been the result of an effort to get away from nature. "What! Leave the most important relation into which a man can enter to the mercy of chance, when a mere gesture may arouse passion, or the color of a corsage induce desire! No, you English, you who are so self-controlled, you are not going seriously to defend that! You talk of love as though it lasted for ever. You talk of sacrificing to love; but what you really sacrifice, or risk sacrificing, is the whole of the latter part of married existence for the sake of the first two or three years. Marriage is not one long honeymoon. We wish it were. When you agree to a marriage you fix your eyes on the honeymoon. When we agree to a marriage we try to see it as it will be five or ten years hence. We assert that, in the average instance, five years after the wedding it doesn't matter whether or not the parties were in love on the wedding-day. Hence we will not yield to the gusts of the moment. Your system is, moreover, if we may be permitted the observation, a premium on improvidence; it is, to some extent, the result of improvidence. You can marry your daughters without dowries, and the ability to do so tempts you to neglect your plain duty to your daughters, and you do not always resist the temptation. Do your marriages of 'romance' turn out better than our marriages of prudence, of careful thought, of long foresight? We do not think they do."

So much for the two ways. Patriotism being the last refuge of a scoundrel, according to Doctor Johnson, I have no intention of judging between them, as my heart prompts me to do, lest I should be accused of it. Nevertheless, I may hint that, while perfectly convinced by the admirable logic of the French, I am still, with the charming illogicalness of the English, in favor of romantic marriages (it being, of course, understood that dowries _ought_ to be far more plentiful than they are in England). If a

Frenchman accuses me of being ready to risk sacrificing the whole of the latter part of married life for the sake of the first two or three years, I would unhesitatingly reply: "Yes, I _am_ ready to risk that sacrifice. I reckon the first two or three years are worth it." But, then, I am English, and therefore romantic by nature. Look at London, that city whose outstanding quality is its romantic quality; and look at the Englishwomen going their ways in the wonderful streets thereof! Their very eyes are full of romance. They may, they do, lack "chic", but they are heroines of drama. Then look at Paris; there is little romance in the fine right lines of Paris. Look at the Parisiennes. They are the most astounding and adorable women yet invented by nature. But they aren't romantic, you know. They don't know what romance is. They are so matter-of-fact that when you think of their matter-of-factness it gives you a shiver in the small of your back.

To return. One may view the two ways in another light. Perhaps the difference between them is, fundamentally, less a difference between the ideas of two races than a difference between the ideas of two "times of life"; and in France the elderly attitude predominates. As people get on in years, even English people, they are more and more in favor of the marriage of reason as against the marriage of romance. Young people, even French people, object strongly to the theory and practice of the marriage of reason. But with them the unique and precious ecstasy of youth is not past, whereas their elders have forgotten its savor. Which is right? No one will ever be able to decide. But neither the one system nor the other will apply itself well to all or nearly all cases. There have been thousands of romantic marriages in England of which it may be said that it would have been better had the French system been in force to prevent their existence. And, equally, thousands of possible romantic marriages have been prevented in France which, had the English system prevailed there, would have turned out excellently. The prevalence of dowries in England would not render the English system perfect (for it must be remembered that money is only one of several ingredients in the French marriage), but it would considerably improve it. However, we are not a provident race, and we are not likely to become one. So our young men must reconcile themselves to the continued absence of dowries.

The reader may be excused for imagining that I am at the end of my remarks. I am not. All that precedes is a mere preliminary to what follows. I want to regard the case of the man who has given the English system a fair trial and found it futile. Thus, we wait on chance in England. We wait for love to arrive. Suppose it doesn't arrive? Where is the English system then? Assume that a man in a position to marry reaches thirty-five or forty without having fallen in love. Why should he not try the French system for a change? Any marriage is better than none at all. Naturally, in England, he couldn't go up to the Chosen Fair and announce: "I am not precisely in love with you, but will you marry me?" He would put it differently. And she would understand. And do you think she would refuse?

Chapter VI

Books

THE PHYSICAL SIDE

The chief interest of many of my readers is avowedly books; they may, they probably do, profess other interests, but they are primarily "bookmen," and when one is a bookman one is a bookman during about twenty-three and three-quarter hours in every day. Now, bookmen are capable of understanding things about books which cannot be put into words; they are not like mere subscribers to circulating libraries; for them a book is not just a book--it is a "book". If these lines should happen to catch the eye of any persons not bookmen, such persons may imagine that I am writing nonsense; but I trust that the bookmen will comprehend me. And I venture, then, to offer a few reflections upon an aspect of modern bookishness that is becoming more and more "actual" as the enterprise of publishers and the beneficent effects of education grow and increase together. I refer to "popular editions" of classics.

Now, I am very grateful to the devisers of cheap and handy editions. The first book I ever bought was the first volume of the first modern series of presentable and really cheap reprints, namely, Macaulay's "Warren Hastings," in "Cassell's National Library" (sixpence, in cloth). That foundation stone of my library has unfortunately disappeared beneath the successive deposits, but another volume of the same series, F.T. Palgrave's

"Visions of England" (an otherwise scarce book), still remains to me through the vicissitudes of seventeen years of sale, purchase, and exchange, and I would not care to part with it. I have over two hundred volumes of that inestimable and incomparable series, "The Temple Classics," besides several hundred assorted volumes of various other series. And when I heard of the new "Everyman's Library," projected by that benefactor of bookmen, Mr. J.M. Dent, my first impassioned act was to sit down and write a postcard to my bookseller ordering George Finlay's "The Byzantine Empire," a work which has waited sixty years for popular recognition. So that I cannot be said to be really antagonistic to cheap reprints.

Strong in this consciousness, I beg to state that cheap and handy reprints are "all very well in their way"--which is a manner of saying that they are not the Alpha and Omega of bookishness. By expending L20 yearly during the next five years a man might collect, in cheap and handy reprints, all that was worth having in classic English literature. But I for one would not be willing to regard such a library as a real library. I would regard it as only a cheap edition of a library. There would be something about it that would arouse in me a certain benevolent disdain, even though every volume was well printed on good paper and inoffensively bound. Why? Well, although it is my profession in life to say what I feel in plain words, I do not know that in this connection I _can_ say what I feel in plain words. I have to rely on a sympathetic comprehension of my attitude in the bookish breasts of my readers.

In the first place, I have an instinctive antipathy to a "series." I do not want "The Golden Legend" and "The Essays of Elia" uniformed alike in a regiment of books. It makes me think of conscription and barracks. Even the noblest series of reprints ever planned (not at all cheap, either, nor heterogeneous in matter), the Tudor Translations, faintly annoys me in the mass.

157

Its appearances in a series seems to me to rob a book of something very delicate and subtle in the aroma of its individuality--something which, it being inexplicable, I will not try to explain.

In the second place, most cheap and handy reprints are small in size. They may be typographically excellent, with large type and opaque paper; they may be convenient to handle; they may be surpassingly suitable for the pocket and the very thing for travel; they may save precious space where shelf-room is limited; but they are small in size. And there is, as regards most literature, a distinct moral value in size. Do I carry my audience with me? I hope so. Let "Paradise Lost" be so produced that you can put it in your waistcoat pocket, and it is no more "Paradise Lost." Milton needs a solid octavo form, with stoutish paper and long primer type. I have "Walpole's Letters" in Newnes's "Thin Paper Classics," a marvelous volume of near nine hundred pages, with a portrait and a good index and a beautiful binding, for three and six, and I am exceedingly indebted to Messrs. Newnes for creating that volume. It was sheer genius on their part to do so. I get charming sensations from it, but sensations not so charming as I should get from Mrs. Paget Toynbee's many-volumed and grandiose edition, even aside from Mrs. Toynbee's erudite notes and the extra letters which she has been able to print. The same letter in Mrs. Toynbee's edition would have a higher aesthetic and moral value for me than in the "editionlet" of Messrs. Newnes. The one cheap series which satisfies my desire for size is Macmillan's "Library of English Classics," in which I have the "Travels" of that mythical personage, Sir John Mandeville. But it is only in paying for it that you know this edition to be cheap, for it measures nine inches by six inches by two inches.

And in the third place, when one buys series, one only partially chooses one's books; they are mainly chosen for one by the publisher. And even if they are not chosen for one by the publisher, they are suggested _to_ one by the publisher. Not so does the genuine bookman form his library. The genuine bookman begins by having specific desires. His study of authorities gives him a demand, and the demand forces him to find the supply. He does not let the supply create the demand. Such a state of affairs would be almost humiliating, almost like the _parvenu_ who calls in the wholesale furnisher and decorator to provide him with a home. A library must be, primarily, the expression of the owner's personality.

Let me assert again that I am strongly in favor of cheap series of reprints. Their influence though not the very finest, is indisputably good. They are as great a boon as cheap bread. They are indispensable where money or space is limited, and in travelling. They decidedly help to educate a taste for books that are neither cheap nor handy; and the most luxurious collectors may not afford to ignore them entirely. But they have their limitations, their disadvantages. They cannot form the backbone of a "proper" library. They make, however, admirable embroidery to a library. My own would look rather plain if it was stripped of them.

THE PHILOSOPHY OF BOOK-BUYING

For some considerable time I have been living, as regards books, with the minimum of comfort and decency--with, in fact, the bare necessaries of life, such necessaries being, in my case, sundry dictionaries, Boswell, an atlas, Wordsworth, an encyclopedia, Shakespeare, Whitaker, some De Maupassant, a poetical anthology, Verlaine, Baudelaire, a natural history of my native county, an old directory of my native town, Sir Thomas Browne, Poe, Walpole's Letters, and a book of memoirs that I will not name. A curious list, you will say. Well, never mind! We do not all care to eat beefsteak and chip potatoes off an oak table, with a foaming quart to the right hand. We have our idiosyncrasies. The point is that I existed on the bare necessaries of life (very healthy--doctors say) for a long time. And then, just lately, I summoned energy and caused fifteen hundred volumes to be transported to me; and I arranged them on shelves; and I re-arranged them on shelves; and I left them to arrange themselves on shelves.

Well, you know, the way that I walk up and down in front of these volumes, whose faces I had half-forgotten, is perfectly infantile. It is like the way of a child at a menagerie. There, in its cage, is that 1839 edition of Shelley, edited by Mrs. Shelley, that I once nearly sold to the British Museum because the Keeper of Printed Books thought he hadn't got a copy--only he had! And there, in a cage by himself, because of his terrible hugeness, is the 1652 Paris edition of Montaigne's Essays. And so I might continue, and so I would continue, were it not essential that I come to my argument.

Do you suppose that the presence of these books, after our long separation, is making me read more than I did? Do you suppose I am engaged in looking up my favorite passages? Not a bit. The other evening I had a long tram journey, and, before starting, I tried to select a book to take with me. I couldn't find one to suit just the tram-mood. As I had to _catch_ the tram I was obliged to settle on something, and in the end I went off with nothing more original than "Hamlet," which I am really too familiar with.... Then I bought an evening paper, and read it all through, including advertisements. So I said to myself: "This is a nice result of all my trouble to resume company with some of my books!" However, as I have long since ceased to be surprised at the eccentric manner in which human nature refuses to act as one would have expected it to act, I was able to keep calm and unashamed during this extraordinary experience. And I am still walking up and down in front of my books and enjoying them without reading them.

I wish to argue that a great deal of cant is talked (and written) about reading. Papers such as the "Anthenaeum," which nevertheless I peruse with joy from end to end every week, can scarcely notice a new edition of a classic without expressing, in a grieved and pessimistic tone, the fear that more people buy these agreeable editions than read them. And if it is so? What then? Are we only to buy the books that we read? The question has merely to be thus bluntly put, and it answers itself. All impassioned bookmen, except a few who devote their whole lives to reading, have rows of books on their shelves which they have never read, and which they never will read. I know that I have hundreds such. My eye rests on the works of Berkeley in three volumes, with a preface by the Right Honorable Arthur James Balfour. I cannot conceive the circumstances under which I shall ever read Berkeley; but I do not regret having bought him in a good edition, and I would buy him again if I had him not; for when I look at him some of his virtue passes into me; I am the better for him. A certain aroma of philosophy informs my soul, and I am less crude than I should otherwise be. This is not fancy, but fact.

Taking Berkeley simply as an instance, I will utilize him a little further. I ought to have read Berkeley, you say; just as I ought to have read Spenser, Ben Jonson, George Eliot, Victor Hugo. Not at all. There is no "ought" about it. If the mass of obtainable first-class literature were, as it was perhaps a century ago, not too large to be assimilated by a man of ordinary limited leisure _in_ his leisure and during the first half of his life, then possibly there might be an "ought" about it. But the mass has grown unmanageable, even by those robust professional readers who can "grapple with whole libraries." And I am not a professional reader. I am a writer, just as I might be a hotel-keeper, a solicitor, a doctor, a grocer, or an earthenware manufacturer. I read in my scanty spare time, and I don't read in all my spare time, either. I have other distractions. I read what I feel inclined to read, and I am conscious of no duty to finish a book that I don't care to finish. I read in my leisure, not from a sense of duty, not to improve myself, but solely because it gives me pleasure to read. Sometimes it takes me a month to get through one book. I expect my case is quite an average case. But am I going to fetter my buying to my reading? Not exactly! I want to have lots of books on my shelves because I know they are good, because I know they would amuse me, because I like to look at them, and because one day I might have a caprice to read them. (Berkeley, even thy turn may come!) In short, I want them because I want them. And shall I be deterred from possessing them by the fear of some sequestered and singular person, some person who has read vastly but who doesn't know the difference between a J.S. Muria cigar and an R.P. Muria, strolling in and bullying me with the dreadful query: "Sir, do you read your books?"

Therefore I say: In buying a book, be influenced by two considerations only. Are you reasonably sure that it is a good book? Have you a desire to possess it? Do not be influenced by the probability or the improbability of your reading it. After all, one does read a certain proportion of what one buys. And further, instinct counts. The man who spends half a crown on Stubbs's "Early Plantagenets" instead of going into the Gaiety pit to see "The Spring Chicken," will probably be the sort of man who can suck goodness out of Stubbs's "Early Plantagenets" years before he bestirs himself to read it.

Chapter VII

Success

CANDID REMARKS

There are times when the whole free and enlightened Press of the United Kingdom seems to become strangely interested in the subject of "success," of getting on in life. We are passing through such a period now. It would be difficult to name the prominent journalists who have not lately written, in some form or another, about success. Most singular phenomenon of all, Dr. Emil Reich has left Plato, duchesses, and Claridge's Hotel, in order to instruct the million readers of a morning paper in the principles of success! What the million readers thought of the Doctor's stirring and strenuous sentences I will not imagine; but I know what I thought, as a plain man. After taking due cognizance of his airy play with the "constants" and "variables" of success, after watching him treat "energetics" (his wonderful new name for the "science" of success) as though because he had made it end in "ics" it resembled mathematics, I thought that the sublime and venerable art of mystification could no further go. If my fellow-pilgrim through this vale of woe, the average young man who arrives at Waterloo at 9.40 every morning with a cigarette in his mouth and a second-class season over his heart and vague aspirations in his soul, was half as mystified as I was, he has probably ere this decided that the science of success has all the disadvantages of algebra without any of the advantages of cricket, and that he may as well leave it alone lest evil should befall him. On the off-chance that he has come as yet to no decision about the science of success, I am determined to deal with the subject in a disturbingly candid manner. I feel that it is as dangerous to tell the truth about success as it is to tell the truth about the United States; but being thoroughly accustomed to the whistle of bullets round my head, I will nevertheless try.

Most writers on success are, through sheer goodness of heart, wickedly disingenuous. For the basis of their argument is that nearly any one who gives his mind to it can achieve success. This is, to put it briefly, untrue. The very central idea of success is separation from the multitude of plain men; it is perhaps the only idea common to all the various sorts of success-- differentiation from the crowd. To address the population at large, and tell it how to separate itself from itself, is merely silly. I am now, of course, using the word success in its ordinary sense. If human nature were more perfect than it is, success in life would mean an intimate knowledge of one's self and the achievement of a philosophic inward calm, and such a goal might well be reached by the majority of mortals. But to us success signifies something else. It may be divided into four branches: (1) Distinction in pure or applied science. This is the least gross of all forms of success as we regard it, for it frequently implies poverty, and it does not by any means always imply fame. (2) Distinction in the arts. Fame and adulation are usually implied in this, though they do not commonly bring riches with them. (3) Direct influence and power over the material lives of other men; that is to say, distinction in politics, national or local. (4) Success in amassing money. This last is the commonest and easiest. Most forms of success will fall under one of these heads. Are they possible to that renowned and much-flattered person, the man in the street? They are not, and well you know it, all you professors of the science of success! Only a small minority of us can even become rich.

Happily, while it is true that success in its common acceptation is, by its very essence, impossible to the majority, there is an accompanying truth which adjusts the balance; to wit, that the majority do not desire success. This may seem a bold saying, but it is in accordance with the facts. Conceive the man in the street suddenly, by some miracle, invested with political power, and, of course, under the obligation to use it. He would be so upset, worried, wearied, and exasperated at the end of a week that he would be ready to give the eyes out of his head in order to get rid of it. As for success in science or in art, the average person's interest in such matters is so slight, compared with that of the man of science or the artist, that he cannot be said to have an interest in them. And supposing that distinction in them were thrust upon him he would rapidly lose that distinction by simple indifference and neglect. The average person certainly wants some money, and the average person does not usually rest until he has got as much as is needed for the satisfaction of his instinctive needs. He will move the heaven and earth of his environment to earn sufficient money for marriage in the "station" to which he has been accustomed; and precisely at that point his genuine desire for money will cease to be active. The average man has this in common with the most exceptional genius, that his career in its main contours is governed by his instincts. The average man flourishes and finds his ease in an atmosphere of peaceful routine. Men destined for success flourish and find their ease in an atmosphere of collision and disturbance. The two temperaments are diverse. Naturally the average man dreams vaguely, upon occasion; he dreams how nice it would be to be famous and rich. We all dream vaguely upon such things. But to dream vaguely is not to desire. I often tell myself that I would give anything to be the equal of Cinquevalli, the juggler, or to be the captain of the largest Atlantic liner. But the reflective part of me tells me that my yearning to emulate these astonishing personages is not a genuine desire, and that its realization would not increase my happiness.

To obtain a passably true notion of what happens to the mass of mankind in its progress from the cradle to the grave, one must not attempt to survey a whole nation, nor even a great metropolis, nor even a very big city like Manchester or Liverpool. These panoramas are so immense and confusing that they defeat the observing eye. It is better to take a small town of, say, twenty or thirty thousand inhabitants--such a town as most of us know, more or less intimately. The extremely few individuals whose instincts mark them out to take part in the struggle for success can be identified at once. For the first thing they do is to leave the town. The air of the town is not bracing enough for them. Their nostrils dilate for something keener. Those who are left form a microcosm which is representative enough of the world at large. Between the ages of thirty and forty they begin to sort themselves out. In their own sphere they take their places. A dozen or so politicians form the town council and rule the town. Half a dozen business men stand for the town's commercial activity and its wealth. A few others teach science and art, or are locally known as botanists, geologists, amateurs of music, or amateurs of some other art. These are the distinguished, and it will be perceived that they cannot be more numerous than they are. What of the rest? Have they struggled for success and been beaten? Not they. Do they, as they grow old, resemble disappointed men? Not they. They have fulfilled themselves modestly. They have got what they genuinely tried to get. They have never even gone near the outskirts of the battle for success. But they have not failed. The number of failures is surprisingly small. You see a shabby, disappointed, ageing man flit down the main street, and someone replies to your inquiry: "That's So-and-so, one of life's failures, poor fellow!" And the very tone in which the words are uttered proves the excessive rarity of the real failure. It goes without saying that the case of the handful who have left the town in search of the Success with the capital S has a tremendous interest of curiosity for the mass who remain. I will consider it.

THE SUCCESSFUL AND THE UNSUCCESSFUL

Having boldly stated that success is not, and cannot be, within grasp of the majority, I now proceed to state, as regards the minority, that they do not achieve it in the manner in which they are commonly supposed to achieve it. And I may add an expression of my thankfulness that they do not. The popular delusion is that success is attained by what I may call the "Benjamin Franklin" method. Franklin was a very great man; he united in his character a set of splendid qualities as various, in their different ways, as those possessed by Leonardo da Vinci. I have an immense admiration for him. But his Autobiography does make me angry. His Autobiography is understood to be a classic, and if you say a word against it in the United States you are apt to get killed. I do not, however, contemplate an immediate visit to the United States, and I shall venture to assert that Benjamin Franklin's Autobiography is a detestable book and a misleading book. I can recall only two other volumes which I would more willingly revile. One is _Samuel Budgett: The Successful Merchant_, and the other is _From Log Cabin to White House_, being the history of President Garfield. Such books may impose on boys, and it is conceivable that they do not harm boys (Franklin, by the way, began his Autobiography in the form of a letter to his son), but the grown man who can support them without nausea ought to go and see a doctor, for there is something wrong with him.

"I began now," blandly remarks Franklin, "to have some acquaintance among the young people of the town that were lovers of reading, with whom I spent my evenings very pleasantly; _and gained money by my industry and frugality_." Or again: "It was about this time I conceived the bold and arduous project of arriving at moral perfection.... I made a little book, in which I allotted a page for each of the virtues. I ruled each page with red ink, so as to have seven columns, one for each day of the week.... I crossed these columns with thirteen red lines, marking the beginning of each line with the first letter of one of the virtues; on which line, and in its proper column, I might mark, by a little black spot, every fault I found upon examination to have been committed respecting that virtue, upon that day." Shade of Franklin, where'er thou art, this is really a little bit stiff! A man may be excused even such infamies of priggishness, but truly he ought not to go and write them down, especially to his son. And why the detail about red ink? If Franklin's son was not driven to evil courses by the perusal of that monstrous Autobiography, he must have been a man almost as astounding as his father. Now Franklin could only have written his "immortal classic" from one of three motives: (1) Sheer conceit. He was a prig, but he was not conceited. (2) A desire that others should profit by his mistakes. He never made any mistakes. Now and again he emphasizes some trifling error, but that is "only his fun." (3) A desire that others should profit by the recital of his virtuous sagacity to reach a similar success. The last was undoubtedly his principal motive. Honest fellow, who happened to be a genius! But the point is that his success was in no way the result of his virtuous sagacity. I would go further, and say that his dreadful virtuous sagacity often hindered his success.

No one is a worse guide to success than your typical successful man. He seldom understands the reasons of his own success; and when he is asked by a popular magazine to give his experiences for the benefit of the youth of a whole nation, it is impossible for him to be natural and sincere. He knows the kind of thing that is expected from him, and if he didn't come to London with half a crown in his pocket he probably did something equally silly, and he puts _that_ down, and the note of the article or interview is struck, and good-bye to genuine truth! There recently appeared in a daily paper an autobiographic-didactic article by one of the world's richest men which was the most "inadequate" article of the sort that I have ever come across. Successful men forget so much of their lives! Moreover, nothing is easier than to explain an accomplished fact in a nice, agreeable, conventional way. The entire business of success is a gigantic tacit conspiracy on the part of the minority to deceive the majority.

Are successful men more industrious, frugal, and intelligent than men who are not successful? I maintain that they are not, and I have studied successful men at close quarters. One of the commonest characteristics of the successful man is his idleness, his immense capacity for wasting time. I stoutly assert that as a rule successful men are by habit comparatively idle. As for frugality, it is practically unknown among the successful classes: this statement applies with particular force to financiers. As for intelligence, I have over and over again been startled by the lack of intelligence in successful men. They are, indeed, capable of stupidities that would be the ruin of a plain clerk. And much of the talk in those circles which surround the successful man is devoted to the enumeration of instances of his lack of intelligence. Another point: successful men seldom succeed as the result of an ordered arrangement of their lives; they are the least methodical of creatures. Naturally when they have "arrived" they amuse themselves and impress the majority by being convinced that right from the start, with a steady eye on the goal, they had carefully planned every foot of the route.

No! Great success never depends on the practice of the humbler virtues, though it may occasionally depend on the practice of the prouder vices. Use industry, frugality, and common sense by all means, but do not expect that they will help you to success. Because they will not. I shall no doubt be told that what I have just written has an immoral tendency, and is a direct encouragement to sloth, thriftlessness, etc. One of our chief national faults is our hypocritical desire to suppress the truth on the pretext that to admit it would encourage sin, whereas the real explanation is that we are afraid of the truth. I will not be guilty of that fault. I do like to look a fact in the face without blinking. I am fully persuaded that, per head, there is more of the virtues in the unsuccessful majority than in the successful minority. In London alone are there not hundreds of miles of streets crammed with industry, frugality, and prudence? Some of the most brilliant men I have known have been failures, and not through lack of character either. And some of the least gifted have been marvelously successful. It is impossible to point to a single branch of human activity in which success can be explained by the conventional principles that find general acceptance. I hear you, O reader, murmuring to yourself: "This is all very well, but he is simply being paradoxical for his own diversion." I would that I could persuade you of my intense seriousness! I have endeavored to show what does not make success. I will next endeavor to show what does make it. But my hope is forlorn.

THE INWARDNESS OF SUCCESS

Of course, one can no more explain success than one can explain Beethoven's C minor symphony. One may state what key it is written in, and make expert reflections upon its form, and catalogue its themes, and relate it to symphonies that preceded it and symphonies that followed it, but in the end one is reduced to saying that the C minor symphony is beautiful--because it is. In the same manner one is reduced to saying that the sole real difference between success and failure is that success succeeds. This being frankly admitted at the outset, I will allow myself to assert that there are three sorts of success. Success A is the accidental sort. It is due to the thing we call chance, and to nothing else. We are all of us still very superstitious, and the caprices of chance have a singular effect upon us. Suppose that I go to Monte Carlo and announce to a friend my firm conviction that red will turn up next time, and I back red for the maximum and red does turn up; my friend, in spite of his intellect, will vaguely attribute to me a mysterious power. Yet chance alone would be responsible. If I did that six times running all the players at the table would be interested in me. If I did it a dozen times all the players in the Casino would regard me with awe. Yet chance alone would be responsible. If I did it eighteen times my name would be in every newspaper in Europe. Yet chance alone would be responsible. I should be, in that department of human activity, an extremely successful man, and the vast majority of people would instinctively credit me with gifts that I do not possess.

If such phenomena of superstition can occur in an affair where the agency of chance is open and avowed, how much more probable is it that people should refuse to be satisfied with the explanation of "sheer accident" in affairs where it is to the interest of the principal actors to conceal the role played by chance! Nevertheless, there can be no doubt in the minds of persons who have viewed success at close quarters that a proportion of it is due solely and utterly to chance. Successful men flourish to-day, and have flourished in the past, who have no quality whatever to differentiate them from the multitude. Red has turned up for them a sufficient number of times, and the universal superstitious instinct not to believe in chance has accordingly surrounded them with a halo. It is merely ridiculous to say, as some do say, that success is never due to chance alone. Because nearly everybody is personally acquainted with reasonable proof, on a great or a small scale, to the contrary.

The second sort of success, B, is that made by men who, while not gifted with first-class talents, have, beyond doubt, the talent to succeed. I should describe these men by saying that, though they deserve something, they do not deserve the dazzling reward known as success. They strike us as overpaid. We meet them in all professions and trades, and we do not really respect them. They excite our curiosity, and perhaps our envy. They may rise very high indeed, but they must always be unpleasantly conscious of a serious reservation in our attitude towards them. And if they could read their obituary notices they would assuredly discern therein a certain chilliness, however kindly we acted up to our great national motto of _De mortuis nil nist bunkum_. It is this class of success which puzzles the social student. How comes it that men without any other talent possess a mysterious and indefinable talent to succeed? Well, it seems to me that such men always display certain characteristics. And the chief of these characteristics is the continual, insatiable _wish_ to succeed. They are preoccupied with the idea of succeeding. We others are not so preoccupied. We dream of success at intervals, but we have not the passion for success. We don't lie awake at nights pondering upon it.

The second characteristic of these men springs naturally from the first. They are always on the look-out. This does not mean that they are industrious. I stated in a previous article my belief that as a rule successful men are not particularly industrious. A man on a raft with his shirt for a signal cannot be termed industrious, but he will keep his eyes open for a sail on the horizon. If he simply lies down and goes to sleep he may miss the chance of his life, in a very special sense. The man with the talent to succeed is the man on the raft who never goes to sleep. His indefatigable orb sweeps the main from sunset to sunset. Having sighted a sail, he gets up on his hind legs and waves that shirt in so determined a manner that the ship is bound to see him and take him off. Occasionally he plunges into the sea, risking sharks and other perils. If he doesn't "get there," we hear nothing of him. If he does, some person will ultimately multiply by ten the number of sharks that he braved: that person is called a biographer.

Let me drop the metaphor. Another characteristic of these men is that they seem to have the exact contrary of what is known as common sense. They will become enamored of some enterprise which infallibly impresses the average common-sense person as a mad and hopeless enterprise. The average common-sense person will demolish the hopes of that enterprise by incontrovertible argument. He will point out that it is foolish on the face of it, that it has never been attempted before, and that it responds to no need of humanity. He will say to himself: "This fellow with his precious enterprise has a twist in his brain. He can't reply to my arguments, and yet he obstinately persists in going on." And the man destined to success does go on. Perhaps the enterprise fails; it often fails; and then the average common-sense person expends much breath in "I told you so's." But the man continues to be on the look-out. His thirst is unassuaged; his taste for enterprises foredoomed to failure is incurable. And one day some enterprise foredoomed to failure develops into a success. We all hear of it. We all open our mouths and gape. Of the failures we have heard nothing. Once the man has achieved success, the thing becomes a habit with him. The difference between a success and a failure is often so slight that a reputation for succeeding will ensure success, and a reputation for failing will ensure failure. Chance plays an important part in such careers, but not a paramount part. One can only say that it is more useful to have luck at the beginning than later on. These "men of success" generally have pliable temperaments. They are not frequently un-moral, but they regard a conscience as a good servant and a bad master. They live in an atmosphere of compromise.

There remains class C of success--the class of sheer high merit. I am not a pessimist, nor am I an optimist. I try to arrive at the truth, and I should say that in putting success C at ten per cent. of the sum total of all successes, I am being generous to class C. Not that I believe that vast quantities of merit go unappreciated. My reason for giving to Class C only a modest share is the fact that there is so little sheer high merit. And does it not stand to reason that high merit must be very exceptional? This sort of success needs no explanation, no accounting for. It is the justification of our singular belief in the principle of the triumph of justice, and it is among natural phenomena perhaps the only justification that can be advanced for that belief. And certainly when we behold the spectacle of genuine distinguished merit gaining, without undue delay and without the sacrifice of dignity or of conscience, the applause of the kind-hearted but obtuse and insensible majority of the human race, we have fair reason to hug ourselves.

Chapter VIII

The Petty Artificialities

The phrase "petty artificialities," employed by one of the correspondents in the great Simple Life argument, has stuck in my mind, although I gave it a plain intimation that it was no longer wanted there. Perhaps it sheds more light than I had at first imagined on the mental state of the persons who use it when they wish to arraign the conditions of "modern life." A vituperative epithet is capable of making a big show. "Artificialities" is a sufficiently scornful word, but when you add "petty" you somehow give the quietus to the pretensions of modern life. Modern life had better hide its diminished head, after that. Modern life is settled and done for--in the opinion of those who have thrown the dart. Only it isn't done for, really, you know. "Petty," after all, means nothing in that connexion. Are there, then, artificialities which are not "petty," which are noble, large, and grand? "Petty" means merely that the users of the word are just a little cross and out of temper. What they think they object to is artificialities of any kind, and so to get rid of their spleen they refer to "petty" artificialities. The device is a common one, and as brilliant as it is futile. Rude adjectives are like blank cartridge. They impress a vain people, including the birds of the air, but they do no execution.

At the same time, let me admit that I deeply sympathize with the irritated users of the impolite phrase "petty artificialities." For it does at any rate show a "divine discontent"; it does prove a high dissatisfaction with conditions which at best are not the final expression of the eternal purpose. It does make for a sort of crude and churlish righteousness. I well know that feeling which induces one to spit out savagely the phrase "petty artificialities of modern life." One has it usually either on getting up or on going to bed. What a petty artificial business it is, getting up, even for a male! Shaving! Why shave? And then going to a drawer and choosing a necktie. Fancy an immortal soul, fancy a fragment of the eternal and indestructible energy, which exists from everlasting to everlasting, deliberately expending its activity on the choice of a necktie! Why a necktie? Then one goes downstairs and exchanges banal phrases with other immortals. And one can't start breakfast immediately, because some sleepy mortal is late.

Why babble? Why wait? Why not say straight out: "Go to the deuce, all of you! Here it's nearly ten o'clock, and me anxious to begin living the higher life at once instead of fiddling around in petty artificialities. Shut up, every one of you. Give me my bacon instantly, and let me gobble it down quick and be off. I'm sick of your ceremonies!" This would at any rate not be artificial. It would save time. And if a similar policy were strictly applied through the day, one could retire to a well-earned repose in the full assurance that the day had been simplified. The time for living the higher life, the time for pushing forward those vast schemes of self-improvement which we all cherish, would decidedly have been increased. One would not have that maddening feeling, which one so frequently does have when the shades of night are falling fast, that the day had been "frittered away." And yet--and yet--I gravely doubt whether this wholesale massacre of those poor petty artificialities would bring us appreciably nearer the millennium.

For there is one thing, and a thing of fundamental importance, which the revolutionists against petty artificialities always fail to appreciate, and that is the necessity and the value of convention. I cannot in a paragraph deal effectively with this most difficult and complex question. I can only point the reader to analogous phenomena in the arts. All the arts are a conventionalization, an ordering of nature. Even in a garden you put the plants in rows, and you subordinate the well-being of one to the general well-being. The sole difference between a garden and the wild woods is a petty artificiality. In writing a sonnet you actually cramp the profoundest emotional conceptions into a length and a number of lines and a jingling of like sounds arbitrarily fixed beforehand! Wordsworth's "The world is too much with us" is a solid, horrid mass of petty artificiality. Why couldn't the fellow say what he meant and have done with it, instead of making "powers" rhyme with "ours," and worrying himself to use exactly a hundred and forty syllables? As for music, the amount of time that must have been devoted to petty artificiality in the construction of an affair like Bach's Chaconne is simply staggering. Then look at pictures, absurdly confined in frames, with their ingenious contrasts of light and shade and mass against mass. Nothing but petty artificiality! In other words, nothing but "form"--"form" which is the basis of all beauty, whether material or otherwise.

Now, what form is in art, conventions (petty artificialities) are in life. Just as you can have too much form in art, so you can have too much convention in life. But no art that is not planned in form is worth consideration, and no life that is not planned in convention can ever be satisfactory. Convention is not the essence of life, but it is the protecting garment and preservative of life, and it is also one very valuable means by which life can express itself. It is largely symbolic; and symbols, while being expressive, are also great time-savers. The despisers of petty artificialities should think of this. Take the striking instance of that pettiest artificiality, leaving cards. Well, searchers after the real, what would you substitute for it? If you dropped it and substituted nothing, the result would tend towards a loosening of the bonds of society, and it would tend towards the diminution of the number of your friends. And if you dropped it and tried to substitute something less artificial and more real, you would accomplish no more than you accomplish with cards, you would inconvenience everybody, and waste a good deal of your own time. I cannot too strongly insist that the basis of convention is a symbolism, primarily meant to display a regard for the feelings of other people. If you do not display a regard for the feelings of other people, you may as well go and live on herbs in the desert. And if you are to display such a regard you cannot do it more expeditiously, at a smaller outlay of time and brains, than by adopting the code of convention now generally practised. It comes to this--that you cannot have all the advantages of living in the desert while you are living in a society. It would be delightful for you if you could, but you can't.

There are two further reasons for the continuance of conventionality. And one is the mysterious but indisputable fact that the full beauty of an activity is never brought out until it is subjected to discipline and strict ordering and nice balancing. A life without petty artificiality would be the life of a tiger in the forest. A beautiful life, perhaps, a life of "burning bright," but not reaching the highest ideal of beauty! Laws and rules, forms and ceremonies are good in themselves, from a merely aesthetic point of view, apart from their social value and necessity.

And the other reason is that one cannot always be at the full strain of "self-improvement," and "evolutionary progress," and generally beating the big drum. Human nature will not stand it. There is, if we will only be patient, ample time for the "artificial" as well as for the "real." Those persons who think that there isn't, ought to return to school and learn arithmetic. Supposing that all "petty artificialities" were suddenly swept away, and we were able to show our regard and consideration for our fellow creatures by the swift processes of thought alone, we should find ourselves with a terrible lot of time hanging heavy on our hands. We can no more spend all our waking hours in consciously striving towards higher things than we can dine exclusively off jam. What frightful prigs we should become if we had nothing to do but cultivate our noblest faculties! I beg the despisers of artificiality to reflect upon these observations, however incomplete these observations may be, and to consider whether they would be quite content if they got what they are crying out for.

Chapter IX

The Secret of Content

I have said lightly a propos of the conclusion arrived at by several correspondents and by myself that the cry for the simple life was merely a new form of the old cry for happiness, that I would explain what it was that made life worth living for me. The word has gone forth, and I must endeavor to redeem my promise. But I do so with qualms and with diffidence. First, there is the natural instinct against speaking of that which is in the core of one's mind. Second, there is the fear, nearly amounting to certainty, of being misunderstood or not comprehended at all. And third, there is the absurd insufficiency of space. However, for me, spiritual content (I will not use the word "happiness," which implies too much) springs essentially from no mental or physical facts. It springs from the spiritual fact that there is something higher in man than the mind, and that that something can control the mind. Call that something the soul, or what you will. My sense of security amid the collisions of existence lies in the firm consciousness that just as my body is the servant of my mind, so is my mind the servant of "me." An unruly servant, but a servant--and possibly getting less unruly every day! Often have I said to that restive brain: "Now, O mind, sole means of communication between the divine _me_ and all external phenomena, you are not a free agent; you are a subordinate; you are nothing but a piece of machinery; and obey me you _shall_."

The mind can only be conquered by regular meditation, by deciding beforehand what direction its activity ought to take, and insisting that its activity takes that direction; also by never leaving it idle, undirected, masterless, to play at random like a child in the streets after dark. This is extremely difficult, but it can be done, and it is marvelously well worth doing. The fault of the epoch is the absence of meditativeness. A sagacious man will strive to correct in himself the faults of his epoch. In some deep ways the twelfth century had advantages over the twentieth. It practiced meditation. The twentieth does Sandow exercises. Meditation (I speak only for myself) is the least dispensable of the day's doings. What do I force my mind to meditate upon? Upon various things, but chiefly upon one.

Namely, that Force, Energy, Life--the Incomprehensible has many names--is indestructible, and that, in the last analysis, there is only one single, unique Force, Energy, Life. Science is gradually reducing all elements to one element. Science is making it increasingly difficult to conceive matter apart from spirit. Everything lives. Even my razor gets "tired." And the fatigue of my razor is no more nor less explicable than my fatigue after a passage of arms with my mind. The Force in it, and in me, has been transformed, not lost. All Force is the same force. Science just now has a tendency to call it electricity; but I am indifferent to such baptisms. The same Force pervades my razor, my cow in my field, and the central _me_ which dominates my mind: the same force in different stages of evolution. And that Force persists forever. In such paths do I compel my mind to walk daily. Daily it has to recognize that the mysterious Ego controlling it is a part of that divine Force which exists from everlasting to everlasting, and which, in its ultimate atoms, nothing can harm. By such a course of training, even the mind, the coarse, practical mind, at last perceives that worldly accidents don't count.

"But," you will exclaim, "This is nothing but the immortality of the soul over again!" Well, in a slightly more abstract form, it is. (I never said I had discovered anything new.) I do not permit myself to be dogmatic about the persistence of personality, or even of individuality after death. But, in basing my physical and mental life on the assumption that there is something in me which is indestructible and essentially changeless, I go no further than science points. Yes, if it gives you pleasure, let us call it the immortality of the soul. If I miss my train, or my tailor disgraces himself, or I lose that earthly manifestation of Force that happens to be dearest to me, I say to my mind: "Mind, concentrate your powers upon the full realization of the fact that I, your master, am immortal and beyond the reach of accidents." And my mind, knowing by this time that I am a hard master, obediently does so. Am I, a portion of the Infinite Force that existed billions of years ago, and which will exist billions of years hence, going to allow myself to be worried by any terrestrial physical or mental event? I am not. As for the vicissitudes of my body, that servant of my servant, it had better keep its place, and not make too much fuss. Not that any fuss occurring in either of these outward envelopes of the eternal _me_ could really disturb me. The eternal is calm; it has the best reason for being so.

So you say to yourselves: "Here is a man in a penny weekly paper advocating daily meditation upon the immortality of the soul as a cure for discontent and unhappiness! A strange phenomenon!" That it should be strange is an indictment of the epoch. My only reply to you is this: Try it. Of course, I freely grant that such meditation, while it "casts out fear," slowly kills desire and makes for a certain high indifference; and that the extinguishing of desire, with an accompanying indifference, be it high or low, is bad for youth. But I am not a youth, and to-day I am writing for those who have tasted disillusion: which youth has not. Yet I would not have you believe that I scorn the brief joys of this world. My attitude towards them would fain be that of Socrates, as stated by the incomparable Marcus Aurelius: "He knew how to lack, and how to enjoy, those things in the lack whereof most men show themselves weak; and in the fruition, intemperate."

Besides commanding my mind to dwell upon the indestructibly and final omnipotence of the Force which is me, I command it to dwell upon the logical consequence of that "unity of force" which science is now beginning to teach. The same essential force that is "me" is also "you". Says the Indian proverb: "I met a hundred men on the road to Delhi, and they were all my brothers." Yes, and they were all my twin brothers, if I may so express it, and a thousand times closer to me even than the common conception of twin brothers. We are all of us the same in essence; what separates us is merely differences in our respective stages of evolution. Constant reflection upon this fact must produce that universal sympathy which alone can produce a positive content. It must do away with such ridiculous feelings as blame, irritation, anger, resentment. It must establish in the mind an all-embracing tolerance. Until a man can look upon the drunkard in his drunkenness, and upon the wife-beater in his brutality, with pure and calm compassion; until his heart goes out instinctively to every other manifestation of the unique Force; until he is surcharged with an eager and unconquerable benevolence towards everything that lives; until he has utterly abandoned the presumptuous practice of judging and condemning--he will never attain real content. "Ah!" you exclaim again, "he has nothing newer to tell us than that 'the greatest of these is charity'!" I have not. It may strike you as excessively funny, but I have discovered nothing newer than that. I merely remind you of it. Thus it is, twins on the road to Delhi, by continual meditation upon the indestructibility of

Force, that I try to cultivate calm, and by continual meditation upon the oneness of Force that I try to cultivate charity, being fully convinced that in calmness and in charity lies the secret of a placid if not ecstatic happiness. It is often said that no thinking person can be happy in this world. My view is that the more a man thinks the more happy he is likely to be. I have spoken. *I am overwhelmingly aware that I have spoken crudely, abruptly, inadequately, confusedly.*

About the Author

Arnold Bennett (1867 – 1931) was an English novelist, playwright, and journalist. Although the majority of his works were fiction, his non-fiction books, which focused in the areas of success and New Thought, have been very influential in the field of personal development.

Made in the USA
Monee, IL
27 February 2022

91942755R00111